DATE DUE

THE COMMONWEALTH AND INTERNATIONAL LIBRARY
Joint Chairman of the Honorary Editorial Advisory Board
SIR ROBERT ROBINSON, O.M., F.R.S., LONDON
DEAN ATHELSTAN SPILHAUS, MINNESOTA
Publisher : ROBERT MAXWELL, M.C., M.P.

COMMONWEALTH AFFAIRS DIVISION
General Editors : SIR KENNETH BRADLEY AND D. TAYLOR

Economic Co-operation in the Commonwealth

A

The Editors of this series accept no responsibility for, and do not necessarily agree with, the views expressed by the authors, whose opinions are their own.

Economic Co-operation in the Commonwealth

by GUY ARNOLD

PERGAMON PRESS

OXFORD · LONDON · EDINBURGH · NEW YORK
TORONTO · SYDNEY · PARIS : BRAUNSCHWEIG

Pergamon Press Ltd., Headington Hill Hall, Oxford
4 & 5 Fitzroy Square, London W.1
Pergamon Press (Scotland) Ltd., 2 & 3 Teviot Place, Edinburgh 1
Pergamon Press Inc., 44–01 21st Street, Long Island City, New York 11101
Pergamon of Canada, Ltd., 6 Adelaide Street East, Toronto, Ontario
Pergamon Press (Aust.) Pty. Ltd., 20–22 Margaret Street,
Sydney, New South Wales
Pergamon Press S.A.R.L., 24 rue des Écoles, Paris 5e
Vieweg & Sohn GmbH, Burgplatz 1, Braunschweig

Copyright © 1967 Pergamon Press Ltd.
First edition 1967
Library of Congress Catalog Card No. 67–18947

Printed in Great Britain by Watmoughs Limited, Idle, Bradford and London

This book is sold subject to the condition
that it shall not, by way of trade, be lent,
resold, hired out, or otherwise disposed
of without the publisher's consent,
in any form of binding or cover
other than that in which
it is published.

(3324/67)

HC
259
A74
1967

Contents

LIST OF MAPS   vii

PREFACE   ix

1. The Economics of Imperialism   1
    Economics and the Growth of Empire   1
    Free Trade and Protection   6
    The First World War   10
    Ottawa 1932: Imperial Preference   13
    Sterling   17

2. The Basis for Economic Co-operation   20
    Factors after the War   20
    The New Commonwealth Emerges   26
    The Beginnings of Aid   29
    Independence   40
    The Question of Bases   50
    Conclusion   51

3. Trade, Sterling and Investment   55
    The Pattern of Commonwealth Trade   57
    Sterling and the Sterling Area   67
    Investment   74

4. Economic Blocs   80
    The Common Market   83
    The United States   89
    Regional Blocs   94

5. Aid   98
    Reasons for Aid   99
    Kinds of Aid   106
    The General Flow of Aid   108
    Commonwealth Needs   111
    The Commonwealth Aid Effort   116
    A Commonwealth Aid Plan   120

6. Neo-colonialism   131

7. Immigration and Minorities   144

8. Future Prospects   161

   BIBLIOGRAPHY   176

   INDEX   179

List of Maps

Independent Commonwealth Countries, 1966   38–39

Economic Areas—Sterling, E.E.C., U.S.A.   70–71

Commonwealth Africa, 1966   134–135

Commonwealth Immigration and Minorities   166–168

Preface

ALTHOUGH this sets out to be an account of economic co-operation in the Commonwealth, the subject of economics is treated as a branch of politics. No doubt this is contrary to much current theory, but it is the opinion of the author that economics are no more than one of several factors influencing the relations between nations and that when political factors—nationalism, questions of race or ideological alignments—have to be considered, they are likely to prove of greater importance than mere economic advantage.

It is for this reason that a good deal of space has been devoted to subjects such as independence, neo-colonialism, immigration and minority problems.

There are a number of links that bind Commonwealth countries together. Although there is some room for discussion it is generally accepted that economic bonds are the most important and practical. Certainly they are the only ones capable of measurement in concrete terms. It is, however, the contention of this book that Commonwealth economic links—like other Commonwealth bonds—are no more than useful political instruments. In themselves they do not justify the existence of the Commonwealth although, of course, they do help to keep the organization together. Consequently they deserve to be fostered and encouraged.

There are a number of critics, particularly in Britain, who no longer believe that the Commonwealth is worth any serious political effort. In the author's opinion they are profoundly wrong. Nonetheless, such critics can present a powerful case always in highly practical terms. Initially they may find some comfort in the theses advanced here for it is a general argument of the book that most Commonwealth economic links would continue to operate even were the Commonwealth to disintegrate.

B

The Commonwealth has grown organically; historically it is the offspring of the British Empire. The various links that exist— economic, or of law, language, custom, consultation—arise naturally out of past British imperial control. They are worth preserving. Anything that helps nations to work together is of value. Nonetheless, a Commonwealth based upon past sentiment will not last long; nor, if it is purely a matter of narrow advantages to its individual members will so oddly assorted a group thrive indefinitely.

Nothing does more damage to a cause than pretending it to be what it is not, and few institutions have suffered so much from this kind of misguided support than has the Commonwealth. However harsh and unpleasant, realities have to be faced. The Commonwealth at present exists somewhat precariously and certain links—often extremely tenuous—help to bind it together. They alone are not enough: some are declining in value with the passage of time; others offer realistic advantages but these would often continue to operate whether or not the association existed. The justification for the Commonwealth must be found elsewhere. It will only continue in the future if it finds a purpose to which all its members can subscribe.

Such a justification lies in the field of international race relations, potentially the most explosive in the world. It is an area in which the Commonwealth as a group possesses unique advantages. If existing links—economic and otherwise—can be used to cement the Commonwealth association they will further a purpose of far greater importance than any immediate advantages individual countries obtain from Commonwealth membership. It is in these terms that economic co-operation in the Commonwealth has been considered.

CHAPTER 1

The Economics of Imperialism

ECONOMICS AND THE GROWTH OF EMPIRE

Already, with the close of the medieval period, England's strength had come increasingly to depend upon its sea trade with Europe and the Mediterranean. The Tudors, under the two Henrys, followed a mercantile policy of protection for the merchant adventurers, the passing of Navigation Acts, and the build-up of naval power that laid the foundations for later economic expansion.

The closing of the old land routes to the East with the coming of the Turks precipitated the 'Age of Discovery'; but, at first, this was dominated by Spain and Portugal. Papal Bulls of 1493 divided the unknown world between the two of them: most of the Americas were allotted to Spanish conquest and expansion; Brazil, Africa and the Indies by the Cape route were reserved for Portugal.

At that time England contented herself with attempts to find the North-West and North-East passages to the Indies; with their land-falls in North America the Cabots began England's connexion with the New World. But the sixteenth century saw the beginnings of modern nationalism in Europe and, inevitably, it was only a question of time before England and France challenged Spain and Portugal across the seas. Commerce, religion, national pride—all ensured a future clash. It came, for England, during Elizabeth I's reign. First the challenge to Spanish trade routes by English sea captains (often no more than pirates) and raids on the Spanish Main—a running, undeclared war. Then, Drake's circumnavigation of the world and mounting attacks upon Spanish and Portuguese seapower until war was declared. The defeat of the Armada climaxed but did not end the war, which dragged on for fifteen more years.

However, the very end of Elizabeth's reign saw the formation of the East India Company. The grant of a royal monopoly charter to merchant adventurers to trade with the East using the Cape route and the sailing of the first East India Company expedition in 1601 opened a new phase of English history and signified the real beginning of the British Empire.

The history of England's imperial growth, the story of British India, the acquisition of African outposts—to safeguard the route to India—and all that followed in the British African Empire have their beginnings with the East India Company. At a later date the search for religious freedom, rivalry with the French and strategic considerations played their part as well. But the demand for trade, the pursuit of wealth and the needs of an island whose growth depended upon mercantile expansion were the root cause of British imperialism. This fact of trade, the restless seeking for commercial advantage, always provided the logic of British expansion and from the time of Elizabeth I onwards dominated the policies Britain adopted for her Empire. The pattern of economic co-operation in the Commonwealth was set long ago. And if Commonwealth evolution in the present century has been the result of breaking the old pattern this process itself serves as a tribute to the binding force of economic motives that forged the old Empire.

The seventeenth century witnessed two new developments: colonies of settlement, and the growth of the Atlantic trade triangle. The Pilgrim Fathers began the English Colonies of Settlement in North America. Later in the century the capture of Jamaica from Spain and the acquisition of other Caribbean islands started the long period of sugar island ascendancy which as late as the Peace of 1763 could see Britain hesitating whether or not to take Guadeloupe in place of Canada.

The old assumption about colonies of settlement was that they were merely extensions of the mother country: no more. As long as this was believed in both Britain and the Americas the Atlantic trade pattern continued: Britain supplied manufactures and collected the slaves from Africa for the islands and America; in return the West Indies supplied sugar, the American colonies other raw materials—

furs, foodstuffs, fish, tobacco. The eighteenth-century struggles between the British, French and Spanish Empires were for the commercial wealth of the West Indies and the Americas, though Britain and France also disputed in the East until the former emerged victorious on the Indian sub-continent.

But the nature of the struggle was altered when the American colonists defied the old concept of Empire and made a bid for their economic independence. Up to the middle of the eighteenth century the American colonies had accepted, grudgingly no doubt, and with increasing evasions, a trade relationship with Britain that made them the suppliers of raw materials. But their growing strength and assurance as settlements and the wealth they commanded meant, sooner or later, that they would challenge the monopoly trade position of the mother country. First and foremost, when it came, the American War of Independence was fought because the mercantile interests in the colonies had determined that they would both manufacture and trade as they wished, not as Britain dictated.

Thus, mercantile considerations sparked off the wars of the eighteenth century; the determination to control their own economic progress led the American colonies into revolt; and Britain's first imperial phase ended in loss and defeat.

Yet in 1783 Britain still had Canada, her Caribbean islands, her foothold in India. Also she had before her the lesson—even if not yet learnt—that, in the long run, colonies of settlement would emulate her and produce their own manufactures. Much further into the future this lesson would have to be applied to other colonies as well: India and then the African Empire.

It is impossible to overestimate how much of Britain's history in the nineteenth and twentieth centuries derives from the eighteenth-century mercantile drive that led to the acquisition of India. The wealth and splendour of India entitled it to be called 'the brightest jewel in the imperial crown'; they also ensured that Britain became a major Asian power and that strategic rather than economic considerations increasingly came to dominate policies of imperial expansion. At the close of the Napoleonic Wars the Cape was retained from the Dutch to safeguard the route to India. Disraeli purchased a major interest in the Suez Canal in 1875 for the same reason. Gladstone, always protesting, became involved first in Egypt, then the Sudan because of the Empire lifeline to India. Heavier involvement in East Africa seemed natural enough since it was halfway to India anyway, and at least one reason for Britain's 'reluctant' protectorate over Uganda was that it controlled the Nile headwaters and thus Egypt, giving a political lever in case of trouble with the Suez lifeline.

Meanwhile the Indian Empire itself became a base for further expansion. It was a Viceroy of India who launched Raffles on the career that brought Singapore and eventually Malaya into the Empire; it was from India that British influence spread into the Persian Gulf; and opium from India became a major instrument in forcing China to 'open up' to the West and trade on Western terms.

In the present century Britain's involvement in the Middle East from Egypt to Iran, often with disastrous results, has been because of India or as a legacy of the earlier policy. Increasingly, however, it became more and more difficult to disentangle economic from strategic considerations or decide which came first: the immensely valuable Eastern trade whose 'lifeline' had to be guarded; or the Indian Empire, a British 'presence' in Asia that had strategic and influence value in its own right, quite apart from trade. The situation was further complicated by the Australian and New Zealand colonies of settlement: not only did they provide new markets for British goods and produce vital raw materials in return, but in time of danger they were vociferous in their demands that the Empire's lifeline should be protected.

Safeguarding 'lifelines' has become a cliché of Empire; the phrase, however, is revealing. The British, it is true, have enjoyed their imperial vanities, their periods of jingoism and Empire mindedness; yet, on the whole, such humours have been short-lived. England never set out consciously to build an empire; she did determine to be strong and recognized that, for her, strength lay in a world-wide system of trade. The acquisition of the Empire followed from this and the imperial lifelines were all trade routes.

It is one of the ironies of British history that after Adam Smith's doctrine of free trade had come to be accepted by Victorian England—even to the point that one school of thought came to regard colonies as burdens to be thrown away—there followed the last great phase of expansion, perhaps the only one that was consciously imperialistic. Yet even Britain's participation in the 'Scramble for Africa' was reluctant, more the result of European pressures and fears as to her rivals' motives—particularly that they might close areas of Africa to British trade if they instead of Britain annexed these areas—than a positive desire to acquire more territory for its own sake. The final establishment of British control over the greater part of southern Africa only came after the discovery of gold and diamonds on the Rand: once more it was a question of commercial interests pushing forward the imperial frontiers.

The span of one generation, 1890–1914, marks the apogee of British imperial power—an age of proconsuls, Kipling, a never-setting sun and certainty. During those few years Britain could justly claim to be the greatest power in the world: her wealth financed development as much in the United States and Latin America as in her own Empire; and her influence was to be felt everywhere. But her rivals in trade, the United States and Germany, were catching up and passing her. The First World War came, not least because Germany had determined to assert equality of power with Britain despite the latter's Empire, and though Germany lost the war she made her point.

By 1914 Canada, Australia, New Zealand and South Africa all had self-government: in varying degrees they had asserted the independence of their fiscal policies, Canada most of all, New Zealand—almost entirely dependent on the British market for the sale of her lamb and dairy products—the least. Yet despite Britain's economic preponderance in these years, increasingly her policy was being shaped by the insistent demands, backed by their growing economic strength, of her very junior Dominion colleagues.

The shock of war—entered as an imperial crusade but dragging on for weary years which sapped and drained the resources of all the participants and threatened the very existence of the Empire—forced upon Britain and the Dominions a close scrutiny of the whole imperial structure. From this, if there did not emerge a policy, at least a pattern of working together in time of crisis was established. Little came afterwards of the grandiose suggestions made during the war, but the possibilities of close co-operation in the Commonwealth were explored and later attempts to find a common economic basis of action could trace their procedure back to this wartime period.

Long before the First World War, however, free trade as opposed to imperial protection had become a major issue between Britain and her Dominions.

FREE TRADE AND PROTECTION

The dream of imperial self-sufficiency was never attained even in the old Empire. Had it been, the Empire would have lost its dynamism and, instead, economic atrophy and decline would have set in. However, the old concept of colonies was straightforward enough: they supplied raw materials or luxury goods unobtainable in the metropolitan country in return for its manufactures. India fell into this pattern though from time to time the imperial power was obliged to resort to expedients to 'persuade' it to take British goods in return for its own. The best example of ideal colonies were the sugar islands of the West Indies. They took slaves and supplied sugar; they had a small planter *élite*—never large enough to be troublesome—but sufficiently rich to provide a market for British manufactures; they did not compete by producing manufactures of their own. What imperial self-sufficiency really meant in the old sense was a whole series of markets ready to buy whatever Britain had to sell in return for providing her with materials or commodities she needed and could not produce. The regulation or expansion of this trade was in the control of the imperial power.

The pattern was broken by the American colonies. They fought and achieved independence so as to regulate their own commerce without restriction from Britain. Imperial preference survived only two generations after the loss of the American colonies. In its place came free trade, now preached with growing fervour by a Britain whose industrial revolution and progress put her ahead of all rivals.

So the Corn Laws and the old Navigation Acts were repealed, and when British statesmen thought of the Empire at all in this new commercial age they preached that it should be united by principles of free trade. As usual, they had forgotten the lessons of the past. It was all very well to propose a free trade Empire when the advantages all lay with Britain's advanced industrial techniques and productive capacity. But like the American colonies before them the other colonies of settlement, led by Canada and Australia, had no intention of leaving the regulation of their economies in Britain's hands. Just at the time when Britain became a convert to the principles of world free trade, so in the 1850's was Canada forcibly asserting her determination to protect her own infant industries.

The last quarter of the nineteenth century which saw the great revival of imperial interest also coincided with growing fears in Britain about the country's pre-eminent position as the leading industrial nation. There were bad times; depressions; agriculture was declining; others were catching up; world markets were not quite so open to whatever Britain had to sell. Other countries were openly nationalist in their economic policies and adopted increasingly protectionist measures. The concept of free trade began to be questioned in some business circles in Britain and there were a few tentative moves towards protection. They amounted to little at first and soon fell away in good times, but world economic conditions were forcing upon Britain a realization that other methods than a policy of free trade which no one else subscribed to might be essential if she were to maintain her commercial pre-eminence.

It was Joseph Chamberlain, the great apostle of free trade, who attempted to reverse Britain's economic policy. Already protectionists had discovered the merits of Empire; now Chamberlain became its champion. The timing was right. Vast new areas had just been added to Britain's overseas possessions (though in defence of these acquisitions Britain argued that she had only expanded her African Empire at all to prevent her European commercial rivals from closing these areas to British and world free trade); and the country had awoken to the glory and extent of its imperial heritage.

At Ottawa in 1894 the self-governing colonies offered imperial preference but the inducements were insufficient to persuade Britain to sacrifice her foreign markets. Free trade principles still ruled but they were weakening.

The next ten years saw a continuing Empire discussion: Empire free trade or imperial preference. Britain argued for the former, but Empire free trade would inevitably condemn the colonies to the permanent status of suppliers of raw materials. Canada and Australia, protecting their own infant industries, would not accept this. Instead they argued for imperial preference but only after Britain and the Empire as a whole had adopted protection; then they could favour each other at the expense of the foreigner. To this Britain said no: her own trade with foreign countries was greater than that with all her colonies. She did not mean to upset it.

While Chamberlain bid seriously for imperial solidarity by means of a unified (and British controlled) economic policy, the self-governing colonies, following (though more cautiously) the example of the American colonies a century before, made plain their determination to pursue their own courses. They were beginning to feel their national identity in other directions; it was failing to face elementary facts about colonial evolution to imagine there could have been any other outcome. Between 1897 and 1906 Canada, South Africa, Australia and New Zealand all initiated tariff preferences of their own. Though arguments for Empire solidarity which everyone was quite prepared to advocate continued and though for a while longer Britain stuck to her policy of free trade the world economic climate was changing.

Generally it is true that Britain and the four self-governing Dominions put each other's interests before those of outsiders, but each individually also put her own interests before those of her Empire partners. So Britain argued for Empire free trade as against the foreigner: this would give her the advantage over her colonies. The colonies argued for protection all round and then the granting of imperial preferences to each other: this would ensure that they could safeguard themselves against Britain. Consequently little progress was achieved. Both sides made minor concessions but the pattern hardly changed. Britain was not yet ready to abandon her free trade principles and when, in the early 1900's, Chamberlain, now a complete convert to a system of imperial protection, proposed radical tariff reforms, all he succeeded in doing was to split the Tory party. At the subsequent election the Liberals were swept back to power. In all the discussions about trade and the Empire it was trade that won. Indeed, as it had been on earlier occasions and as it was to be again in Commonwealth terms much later in the 1960's, whenever a conflict arose between ideas of Empire or Commonwealth solidarity and the economic interests of an individual member of the group it was always the greater ideal that gave way before practical arguments of Britain's or a colony's commercial advantage.

It is worth remembering that with only one or two rare exceptions neither Britain nor her self-governing colonies in the imperial context nor, again, Britain or her Commonwealth partners in more recent years has ever surrendered any of its own economic interests to a broader concept of group advantage. In so far as there existed a single economic policy during imperial days it was precisely because Britain controlled the Empire politically. And even then the earliest penetrations of London's imperial control were made by the self-governing colonies in economic rather than political terms. In the present age of the modern Commonwealth it is often argued that economic co-operation is a major factor of unity. Yet this is true only in the negative sense. Where economic co-operation between Commonwealth countries has provided exact and comparable benefits to both sides, then mutually beneficial agreements have been reached and are justly considered to be factors working for Commonwealth unity; but only because first they were to the economic advantage of the parties concerned. Where on the other hand a Commonwealth country has recognized that its own economic advantage lay outside the Commonwealth framework it has not hesitated to break the pattern. No member of the Commonwealth has willingly sacrificed its individual economic interests for the benefit of a broader ideal of Commonwealth unity or co-operation. This fact must be recognized in order to obtain a clear perspective of both the strength and the weakness of economics as a factor in Commonwealth affairs.

Despite the collapse of Chamberlain's dreams of imperial economic unity and the defeat of the Tories by the free trade Liberals in 1906 growing changes in the world economic pattern and the sharp increase of protectionist policies among the great commercial nations were forcing Britain to review her position more and more seriously. Furthermore, in all the debate about imperial preference and Empire unity the claims put forward that the Empire could be an autarkic body—supplying all its own needs and independent of foreign trade—made no sense. Not only was the trade of the major colonies directed substantially outside the Empire (though the greater part was still within it) but the majority of British trade was outside the Empire. The same was true of Britain's overseas investment though the gap here was far smaller. Of £3,714,661,000 recorded British overseas investments in 1913, £1,779,995,000 were in the Empire, £1,934,660,000 were in foreign countries.

By 1914 approximately 20% of Britain's imports depended upon capital she had invested abroad (as opposed to normal exports of manufactured goods) and it was increasingly clear that her prosperity as a nation could be jeopardized should a major upheaval force her to lose or sell this overseas wealth. The First World War provided such an upheaval.

THE FIRST WORLD WAR

Never before or after the First World War was the same sense of Empire purpose and unity achieved. Although in 1914 the self-governing colonies had gone a long way towards both defining and demanding the full independence within the Commonwealth that was finally achieved by the Statute of Westminster in 1931, at the time there was no question either as to Britain's leadership of the Empire or as to their full and loyal support of it. And once the real danger and long-drawn-out nature of the war had become fully apparent Empire leaders vied with those in Britain to protest their faith in the imperial mission and their determination to make the Empire so strong once the war ended that it could never again be challenged.

Much of the discussion was in terms of imperial economic self-sufficiency; and because of the crisis of the time, the 'backs to the wall' wartime siege mentality, much of it was wildly extravagant and contrary to economic facts both as they were or possibly could be. Imperial xenophobia became the fashion. The Empire must never again place its economy at the mercy of foreign nations; instead, it must make itself self-sufficient. A policy of imperial autarky was one of self-preservation. In Britain a new interest in her vast colonial territories was awakened; had they really been exploited as they should? Could not the proper deployment of British skill and capital (instead of in foreign countries) make the colonies provide the greater markets required by the Empire and the raw materials that Britain needed? The self-governing colonies were no less forward in producing new ideas: largely in terms of how Britain could alter her trade patterns so as to favour their products at the expense of those from foreign countries. And Germany, of course, was to be punished after the war by exclusion not only from the imperial market but from most others as well.

While this war fever lasted it was not difficult to propound new economic theories of Empire; the impracticalities were sidestepped or glossed over. It was one thing to make general statements of intention or desirability; it was quite another matter when precise post-war policies had to be worked out.

Two reports appeared towards the end of the war: that of the Dominions Royal Commission and the Final Report of the Committee on Commercial and Industrial Policy after the War. The first of these (the Dominions Royal Commission) came nearest to proposing imperial self-sufficiency. After reviewing total Empire resources, pleading for greater reciprocity by the Dominions and repeatedly emphasizing the importance of an Empire economic policy, it then proceeded to suggest that the Empire ought to aim at a situation in which it could resist any foreign pressure because it would have control of sufficient raw materials to guarantee its corporate existence.

When, however, the report gets down to the details of implementing such a policy the difficulties at once become apparent. The report divides commodities into three groups: those of which the Empire had a surplus; those in which the Empire was roughly self-sufficient; and those of which the Empire was in short supply. The dangers were clear enough. Under the first category—Empire surplus goods—it would have to be a very compelling policy indeed that prevented the sale of such surpluses to foreign countries with the consequent dependence upon the commercial bargains such countries exacted in return. Thus, it was not to be expected that, for example, Canada would not sell her surplus wheat outside the Empire if she could, even if this meant accepting in exchange goods that otherwise might come from Britain. In such circumstances it was at least suggested, in aggressive economic terms, that the sale of Empire surpluses to foreign countries could be used as a political bargaining counter for their good behaviour. But that was a two-way weapon.

The second category of commodity—that in which the Empire was self-sufficient—presented least problems though demands could clearly change and upset the balance. The third category—commodities in which the Empire was in short supply—led to some ingenious suggestions: that the full resources of the Empire had not yet been explored; that substitutes could be found and so on. But then it had to be admitted that, expedients apart, some commodities would still have to be sought in foreign countries. This necessary dependence upon the foreigner could be safeguarded in part by judicious British investment to control sources of supply and in the piously expressed hope that the various foreign countries upon which the Empire must depend for certain raw materials would never all combine to deny them to the Empire.

The report's suggestions, coming at a time of war crisis when maximum imperial solidarity had been achieved, represent the nearest approach to a policy of Empire self-sufficiency ever attained. They were, however, illusory. They went against too many economic facts and assumed a peacetime approach to economics that was quite contrary to the individual interests of both Britain and the Dominions. Such suggestions could only have been seriously put forward under the crisis pressures of a major war.

The second report, made in 1918 (the Final Report of the Committee on Commercial and Industrial Policy after the War), was more practical and selfish: Britain would be prepared to offer certain imperial preferences but excepted food and raw materials, or, in other words, the commodities which the Dominions most wanted to sell.

The war ended and the self-governing Dominions signed the Peace Treaty individually, so making their practical emergence as independent nations even though their status was not formally ratified for another thirteen years until the passing of the Statute of Westminster in 1931. But in practical terms this was enough. Meanwhile Britain and the Dominions rapidly forgot the brave wartime plans for imperial self-sufficiency and once more pursued their individual economic advantage. Not only did it make good economic sense to do so but it was sound political sense as well. Nothing would have destroyed the Empire as a dynamic and progressive institution more surely than a truly determined attempt to make it autarkic and so ignore the existence of the rest of the world. Such a policy would have been contrary to all the traditions of economic development in both Britain and her colonies. In any case it was impossible.

Thus in fact, once the war was over, although imperial preference made a few small advances and politicians continued to theorize and enthuse over imperial solidarity while pursuing economic policies that were more often than not contrary to their theme, no major changes in the imperial economic pattern took place until the world slump of 1929 and 1930. Up to that point Britain remained basically a free trade country; and the Dominions, according to their various needs, continued to protect their growing industries, search for markets outside the Empire, and demand from Britain trade concessions she was not prepared to grant.

OTTAWA 1932: IMPERIAL PREFERENCE

A steady growth in the demand for imperial preference continued throughout the years between the end of the war and the financial disasters of 1929 and 1930. It was a common theme in the Empire. Many arguments for preference were stated forcibly and passionately at the Imperial Economic Conference in 1923. At the same time, in true keeping with self-governing traditions, the Dominions were careful while asking for concessions to point out that Britain was entirely free to make whatever decisions she wished. They had no intention of surrendering any of their own freedom of action to a greater imperial whole. The consequence in these relatively good years was a few minor moves towards a system of imperial preference but little real progress.

Then came world economic depression. The whole Empire was affected and of the Dominions Canada most of all. The search for economic remedies was urgent. The Dominions renewed their demands for tariff favours in the British market and this time could make them under world-wide crisis conditions. Britain maintained far greater economic stability through the depression than any other major country. In comparison with the United States her index of industrial production fell only twelve points as opposed to thirty-seven; while the volume of her imports, again, fell by only 10% as opposed to an American fall of more than 30%. In consequence for a time hers was the only major economy that could provide any kind of relief to others by a change in her economic practices—although her own problems were acute enough. In their distress the Dominions pressed Britain to adopt a system of imperial preference. This time they got their way.

The British elections in 1931 brought in a government that favoured protectionist measures and at last it seemed possible that Joseph Chamberlain's dreams of imperial unity fostered by a common economic policy had a chance of becoming reality. In 1932 Empire leaders met at Ottawa for an Imperial Economic Conference.

The demand of the time was quite simple: markets. It was also despairing. The world, headed by the United States, was going ever more ruthlessly protectionist. Australia and Canada in particular asked for British reciprocity in the granting of preferences and Britain gave way. So at last Britain abandoned free trade and adopted imperial preference. A series of bilateral Commonwealth agreements were drawn up covering Britain and the Dominions, India and the Colonies. At the same time higher Empire tariffs were erected against foreign goods.

The crisis of world slump led to fundamental changes in the economic relationship of Britain with her dependent colonies. Until then British rule had permitted free trade in the colonies although imperial control had conferred obvious advantages on British shipping and commercial interests. Now the pattern changed. In 1931 Britain went off the gold standard and colonial currencies were directly linked to sterling. And at Ottawa, apart from the self-governing Dominions, Britain also re-introduced after a period of many decades a system of imperial preference for the colonies. Preference quotas on items such as sugar and tin brought the economic fortunes of certain colonies significantly closer to those of Britain.

Despite the crisis that led to the Ottawa agreements and the triumph of the longstanding demands from the Dominions for a system of imperial preference, now that it had been introduced it did less than its advocates had claimed to cure the economic ills of the Commonwealth. The Dominions might demand vociferously and, in this instance, successfully that Britain grant them preferences. They were still as wary as ever of allowing open British competition within their markets to hurt their own growing industries. They still complained of British government aid to its own farmers. And although in 1932 Britain at the insistence of the Dominions had sacrificed foreign markets in order to promote increased Empire trade the results in the following years were hardly of the kind that ardent supporters of imperial preference had led the world to expect. Faced with prohibitive American tariffs at the time of the depression Canada had been foremost in urging Britain to go protectionist at Ottawa. Yet by 1935 she was negotiating new agreements with Washington. India, a large proportion of whose exports went to foreign countries, never felt happy about the Ottawa agreements and was sufficiently powerful that before long she withdrew from them. As at the time of the First World War, so during the economic crisis of the early 1930's the attraction of imperial self-sufficiency and protection at the expense of the foreigner seemed overwhelmingly great. But subsequent events belied the promise. By 1937 the Empire was already retreating from the stand of 1932: talk of imperial customs unions had been

c

replaced by more general demands for a reduction of world tariff barriers as a whole.

Once again, as the crisis receded so too did concepts of imperial economic solidarity. In fact, no one should have been surprised, for such concepts were contrary to the individual economic interests of the different Commonwealth countries and, as always, economic like political nationalism came first.

Nonetheless, following the depression, sterling provided a reasonably stable alternative to gold as an exchange standard. By the late 1930's world economic conditions had improved substantially and were getting back to normal. Then came the Second World War. Once more Britain faced economic siege. Her war effort, especially in economic terms, was more absolute than that of any other belligerent. The sacrifice of export markets, the sale of overseas assets, the war debts incurred, the loss of shipping, all meant that in 1945 Britain faced the post-war period of reconstruction in a state of financial exhaustion. Thus exports in 1945 were only 40% of what they had been in 1938 and many old markets had been lost for good; the merchant shipping fleet had suffered casualties that had reduced it by 30%; sterling debts and liabilities had jumped from £598 million in 1938 to £3694 million and overseas investments had dropped in value from the 1938 figure of £3545 million to £2417 million. In 1914 Britain was the world's greatest creditor nation; in 1945 she had become its greatest debtor nation. What the country needed was a long period of recuperation. Instead it faced an era of insistent and compelling change and was obliged to meet demands that continued to tax almost beyond its limits the country's already overstrained and run-down resources. At home the economy had to meet the requirements of a social revolution; abroad it faced the pressures of the Cold War. And, as if these two factors were not sufficient a challenge, there now followed the great process of change that was to turn the old Empire and self-governing Dominions into the modern Commonwealth. The Dominions again looked to the London money market to finance their own ambitious schemes of post-war development and economic expansion; and independence for India led to a steady drain on the sterling reserves as the successor states drew upon their wartime credits.

Instead of the rest period she needed so urgently after the war Britain found that the demands upon her economy were greater than ever before. And though London now had to take second place to New York as a world financial capital—and a very weak second place at that—the Commonwealth and other countries as well still looked to Britain and the London money market to provide the means for their development needs. Thus in 1945 and ever since the weakness or strength of sterling has been the key factor in Commonwealth economic co-operation.

STERLING

The great power of Britain throughout the nineteenth century and the lead over all other countries that the industrial revolution had given her ensured that London became the financial capital of the world. Sterling provided an alternative to gold as a standard of exchange. Because of this many countries adopted the financial practice of maintaining sterling balances in London and by doing so enhanced still further London's financial pre-eminence.

The currency of Britain's colonies was backed by sterling; later, with self-government they began to develop their own financial institutions. But in the nineteenth century the sterling area grew naturally out of Britain's commercial and industrial supremacy: at first it consisted of Britain and her Empire. But Britain had also become the main source of funds for development in new countries: not just those of the Empire but throughout the world and particularly in the United States and Latin America. Even though the United States passed British production of manufactured goods in the 1880's and Germany did also by 1910 there was no challenge to the position of sterling before 1914.

The First World War seriously undermined the strength of sterling. In four years the United States had become a major creditor nation and New York had emerged as an alternative centre of world finance, though as yet the dollar had not replaced the pound. Instead two financial systems were to exist side by side. In an effort to maintain confidence in sterling and restore the setbacks it had received as a result of the war Britain returned to the gold standard in the mid-1920's. But the result was to overvalue the pound and in 1931 Britain again had to go off the gold standard. It was at this point that the Sterling Bloc was formed: those countries which decided to maintain their currency in terms of sterling rather than gold became members of the Bloc. They consisted at the time of the Dominions (less Canada) and the Empire; later Portugal, the Scandinavian countries, Iran and Latvia joined the Bloc. Britain's relative stability during the slump helped influence this choice. Between 1931 and the outbreak of the Second World War sterling played a principal part in steadying world finance after the shocks of 1929 and 1930. But it was a greatly weakened currency and in crises liable to suffer in comparison with the dollar.

When war came in 1939 Britain took formal action to protect her gold and hard currency reserves by introducing a system of exchange control. Any country that was willing to initiate comparable controls and keep its reserves in sterling in London was not to be affected by the ban on payments to residents outside Britain: they became members of the Sterling Area. As before, the area coincided with the Empire (less Canada which was too closely linked with the American dollar) but in the course of the war other countries, in the Middle East, and the French and Belgian African colonies also joined it.

In India and the Middle East Britain ran up huge sterling debts during the war and by 1945 her liabilities to the countries concerned exceeded £1700 million. Elsewhere she incurred debts or sold assets so that at the war's end she found herself a debtor nation on an unprecedented scale. Unfortunately Britain's weak position was made still worse by American pressures to end the sterling area, to abolish imperial preference and bring about full convertibility. American industry pushed with determination to get into Commonwealth and Empire markets on equal terms with Britain. Consequently an American loan to Britain was made conditional upon steps towards convertibility within one year of the loan and of acceptance of the principle of non-discrimination in international trade.

In 1947 Britain did attempt to make sterling convertible; the operation lasted only five weeks before it had to be suspended: the outflow from the reserves had become so great that the whole economic structure of Britain and the sterling area was endangered, almost disastrously. This first post-war financial crisis—one of a depressing series that have continued with monotonous regularity ever since— demonstrated only too clearly Britain's altered economic circumstances. The year 1966 is the latest for such a sterling crisis. Indeed, so persistent have biennial crises in sterling become that they can now almost be regarded as a normal aspect of the British way of life.

However, it is important to have a clear understanding of the background: first as to economic drives behind the Empire and the consequent formation of a world financial system based on sterling; second, the reasons for British financial weakness in the years after the Second World War. For the strength of Britain and sterling are and must be crucial factors in any Commonwealth efforts at economic co-operation.

Economic co-operation in the Commonwealth is certainly desirable where it can be achieved and the pursuit of such co-operation provides a worthy political objective. But because this is so there is no point in ignoring either economic or political facts and these in combination place severe limits upon the amount of co-operation that is either practicable or will ever be attained. Apart from all political reasons the failure of imperial dreams for a self-sufficient Empire was due simply to the economic dependence of Britain and the old Dominions upon a wider system of trade than anything the Empire could produce on its own. And if this was true in the past, world economic interdependence is even more the case today.

Secondly and still less encouraging is the harsh political fact of national self-interest. No member of the Commonwealth to date has ever seriously allowed co-operation with its partners to stand in the way of its own economic advantage as it has seen this.

It is in the light of this background and confined by these economic and political limitations that economic co-operation in the Commonwealth must be considered.

CHAPTER 2

The Basis for Economic Co-operation

FACTORS AFTER THE WAR

WHEN the Second World War ended, Britain's prestige was enormous: her Empire was intact; her arms everywhere had been successful; Europe regarded her as a liberator; her influence and power were respected throughout the world. At the conference tables she took her place as an equal alongside the United States and Russia. For five years London, in a very real sense, had been the world's foremost capital: the home of governments in exile, the centre of Western military planning, the embattled city that had stood throughout the war as the symbol of freedom.

If, as a result, the British people assumed that the country was an equal in power to the United States and Russia and, in the years that followed, behaved as though this were a fact of international politics the mistake was understandable. Unfortunately it was also contrary to realities. Washington and Moscow had become the real centres of world decisions and behind the triumphs and outward appearances of great power status Britain was faced by acute problems—of economic weakness, of sheer physical exhaustion, of run-down, damaged, or otherwise outmoded housing, factories, equipment.

That she continued to behave as an equal of the United States and Russia is no doubt to her credit, though it is unlikely that national pride could have permitted her to accept any lesser status at the time or for many subsequent years. And possibly because she did assume equality of status with the two 'super' powers she achieved many things that otherwise would not even have been considered as practical policies.

Really, it took Britain ten years, until the Suez fiasco of 1956, before she began fully to accept the logic of her position and its limitations, both in absolute economic terms and in a world of 'super' powers. And because she did take so long to recognize her altered status the policies that she embarked upon were often to have economic consequences which would affect profoundly her relationships with the rest of the Commonwealth. Nonetheless, the more assuredly a nation assumes a particular role, so the more certainly will others accept the stance which is adopted. As a result in this case the Commonwealth expected from Britain an economic lead commensurate with the political role in which she had cast herself.

Despite these political assumptions about Britain's place in the world at the end of the war there were few illusions about her immediate economic plight. The losses of trade, shipping, overseas investment (see above, page 16) and the size of her new wartime debts faced the country in peacetime with the need to continue emergency measures of controls, rationing and austerity that outlasted anything comparable even in the countries of recently occupied western Europe.

With the ending of Lend-Lease Britain was obliged to seek an immediate loan of £1000 million from the United States. The size of the loan (then worth $4000 million) indicated the extent of Britain's financial difficulties. At the same time Canada and Australia, the wealthiest of the Dominions, also made loans to Britain. Apart from the continuation of economic relations that already existed these loans stand out as the first positive acts of Commonwealth cooperation after the war—and so, in the period of the modern Commonwealth. It was significant both of the growing power of the Dominions and of possible future patterns that the end of the war should see emergency loans from Dominions to Britain rather than the other way about.

However, although Britain's power position may have been sadly altered in relation to the United States and Russia this was only part of the story. As far as the rest of the world was concerned Britain was very powerful indeed. And in the Commonwealth, even if the principle of equality had been accepted this did not alter the realities of power and influence. Britain was still in fact the head of the association and regarded as such by even its most independent-minded members. The process of decolonization in Asia and Africa had not yet started and the economies of all the Empire territories were controlled from London. Moreover, the habits of the past were strong and the Dominions looked naturally to Britain for both political and economic leadership before they looked elsewhere. Canada, it is true, was in the dollar area and more closely tied to the United States economically (and in other ways) than to Britain, but for that very reason, so as to counterbalance the enormous preponderance of American influence, it suited her to co-operate closely with Britain. The other Dominions all remained in the sterling area and their economic fortunes were tied to the strength of sterling and the extent of British trade. When they pursued domestic policies of economic expansion they turned first to Britain for immigrants and finance.

The fact that in the late 1940's and through most of the 1950's large numbers of Britons emigrated to the Dominions and colonies of settlement—Canada, Australia, New Zealand, South Africa, Kenya and the Rhodesias—not only strengthened the 'family' bonds of the Commonwealth but materially affected the economic fortunes of the countries concerned. Immigrants took skills, fresh ideas and numbers to the Commonwealth countries; they increased the size and scope of Britain's Commonwealth markets; more debatably, their loss to Britain had effects, possibly significant, upon her internal economic and political problems.

Secondly, the fact that, despite a shaky start and a few painful years, Britain then made a superb economic recovery and London regained much of its former financial pre-eminence meant that according to old habit the Commonwealth countries sought and increasingly obtained on the London money market the loans they needed for their development. Thus, habit combined with a swift British recovery ensured that old patterns of Commonwealth co-operation not only continued but grew and thrived.

Overshadowing British economic weakness after the war, indeed emphasizing it, was American economic strength. During the war years the United States had more than doubled its production; now its wealth dominated the economies of the West. Not only had American political influence and military power burgeoned all over the world but economically both Britain and Europe found themselves dependent upon the generosity of the United States. American aid in the form of a loan propped up the sagging British economy and, later, Marshall Aid started Europe on the road to recovery. The generosity of American assistance made its acceptance easier; it did not diminish awareness of the dependence that such assistance implied.

The export drive, the dollar gap, productivity teams visiting the United States in the search of 'know-how', the desperate British search for economic strength that would make the country independent of American aid form a vital chapter of British economic history in the post-war era. Only when Britain began sufficiently to emerge from this state of dollar dependency as her own economic strength re-asserted itself did it again make sense to talk of Commonwealth economic co-operation in terms other than purely negative ones of holding together the sterling area and supporting the pound.

The story of the British economy from 1945 to 1949 emphasizes only too clearly her weakness and the extent to which the fortunes of the pound were tied to those of the dollar. Lend-Lease ended in 1945 and was replaced by a £1000 million American loan; in 1947 Britain attempted the convertibility of sterling into dollars but after five weeks and an unprecedented run on the pound was obliged to stop the experiment—and a major financial crisis followed; early in 1948 the American loan came to an end, though soon afterwards Britain benefited from the Marshall Plan and a fresh influx of aid dollars; in 1949 the pound was devalued as against the dollar from $4·03 to $2·80. This was not a happy financial period for Britain; it was, however, one of necessary re-adjustment to the hard facts of economic life. Only when Britian began to cut her political aims a little more according to her economic strength did she manage to achieve greater influence in economic affairs.

The other major factor of the immediate post-war years which was to play a crucial part in shaping British economic policy was the coming of the Cold War. British response to Cold War pressures and her subsequent policies—re-armament, mutual security pacts, military alliances and the maintenance of bases round the world— have been responsible for defence programmes of unprecedented peacetime size which have strained the British economy ever since.

Politically Britain saw the dangers of the Russian threat to Europe before the United States and was in the forefront organizing Western resistance to communism. From 1945 to 1947 she underwrote the economies of both Greece and Turkey until the financial crisis of the latter year forced her to abandon the effort and ask the United States to take it over from her; she played a major part in the Berlin airlift; and her lead in Europe was decisive in bringing NATO into being. Later she played the key role in establishing both the Baghdad Pact (subsequently CENTO) and SEATO. The fact of her Empire meant that she already possessed military bases round the world: the Cold War ensured that she kept them up to strength, increased their size and efficiency or created new ones. In subsequent years the wide-spread network of British overseas bases has been one of the most consistent drains upon the economy of the country, and the attempt to remain a world military power long after the need to do so had passed (quite apart from economic ability to sustain the role) has fettered and reduced Britain's capability of doing other and more useful things with her resources.

In the early days of the Cold War, however, the lead taken by Britain—over Berlin, in NATO and the other Pacts, in Korea— helped maintain her great power status and influence. Because the Dominions—Canada, Australia, New Zealand and South Africa— approved and actively supported the general Western stand in the Cold War Britain's lead was warmly endorsed by them; in consequence her actions enhanced her position of leadership, at least with the old Commonwealth, and gave to her strong bargaining arguments for their support in economic matters. And this she certainly needed from time to time. The possibility of Russian aggression, representing an apparent threat to the whole Western world, drew Britain and the Dominions—especially Australia and New Zealand in their Pacific isolation—more closely together. They again found themselves thinking in terms of wartime co-operation.

In Commonwealth terms Britain still enjoyed an overwhelming power preponderance although, even here, American dominance was only too apparent. Canada came to establish special military defence arrangements with the United States in NORAD; Australia and New Zealand entered into the ANZUS Pact with her.

In summary four main influences worked upon Britain in the immediate post-war period: her determination to remain a great power; the Commonwealth habit of looking to her for leadership; the painful realization of American dominance in world affairs and her need to rely upon both American economic aid and military protection; and the effect of the Cold War in shaping subsequent British military and economic policies. These factors provided the guidelines as well as setting the limitations that have largely determined British foreign policy ever since. The Commonwealth was equally affected by these events. Economics cannot be treated in a vacuum; they are part of a wider political whole. British freedom to manoeuvre, as much as that of her Commonwealth partners, has been circumscribed by these challenges of the post-war years ever since.

It makes little sense to embark upon a discussion of Commonwealth co-operation without first placing economics in the wider perspective of world politics. Defence must be the first consideration of any national government; inevitably, therefore, economic considerations will be bounded by facts of political and military survival. When assessing the possibilities of Commonwealth economic co-operation and the extent to which it makes practical political sense it should not be forgotten that Canada's defence and economy are irretrievably bound up with those of the United States; nor that in 1951 Australia and New Zealand felt compelled to break the old imperial tradition and conclude the ANZUS Pact with the United States and without Britain.

Only after accepting these harsh realities of power does it then make sense to gauge the actual and speculate upon the potential degree of economic co-operation that is either desirable or attainable within the Commonwealth.

THE NEW COMMONWEALTH EMERGES

The granting of independence to British India in 1947 was an event of dual significance: it marked both the end of the old imperial phase and the start of the new Commonwealth. Until that year the Commonwealth consisted of Britain and the white Dominions—the old colonies of settlement. And though in theory it had long been assumed that one day India would achieve independence—back in the 1830's Macaulay had said that when the day came it would be the proudest in English history—in practice large sections of the British public were far from willing to acknowledge either that India was ready for independence or to welcome her as an equal into what so far had been the all-white Commonwealth 'Club'. India had always been a special case—its vast population and continental size if nothing else had ensured that; ever since the 'Mutiny' and the assumption of direct British rule with the passing of the Government of India Act in 1858 it had had its own Secretary of State; and since the First World War it had in many respects been treated on a par with the Dominions.

Few passages in recent British parliamentary history, however, can have been more passionate than the debates leading up to Indian Independence in 1947; and the opposition was headed by Winston Churchill. He was, of course, wrong to oppose, yet it is easy to understand why he did so. With an historian's instinct he saw only too clearly how the momentous act of granting independence marked the end of British imperial power. Once done, the Empire was indeed over since Britain would be surrendering control of the one area that still entitled her in real power terms to claim equality of status with the United States and Russia. As long as Britain remained in India and controlled its economy and the Indian army she had a major, indeed decisive, presence in Asia. When she surrendered that control she returned to the status of a powerful European nation but no more. By comparison her African possessions did not render her a tithe of the power she derived from India.

Suddenly the nature of the Commonwealth had been transformed. Instead of Britain and the four white Dominions of settlement— Canada, Australia, New Zealand and South Africa (which in political terms counted as white), with their leaders acting together from time to time as a 'family' group, and this despite the racial tensions that arose periodically in Canada with clashes between the French- and the English-speaking groups, or the far more serious racial antagonisms between Briton and Boer in South Africa—there was now a Commonwealth that also included India and Pakistan, to be joined a year later by Ceylon. Politically it lay in the balance for nearly two years whether India would remain in the Commonwealth at all. Had she simply opted for Independence there could hardly have developed the new multiracial Commonwealth as it now exists. South Africa would have been glad to see her go since her presence on a basis of equality with the white Dominions struck a decisive blow at the whole validity of the apartheid concept.

It has been argued that Britain allowed, almost encouraged, Burma to seek independence outside the Commonwealth so as to demonstrate the genuinely free nature of the association and reassure India. Perhaps this is an over-subtle interpretation of events. At any rate India stayed and in 1949 took another historic step by becoming a Republic and simply recognizing the King as head of the Commonwealth, so paving the way for the majority of the African and other colonies a decade and more later.

Although this is an account of Commonwealth economic co-operation it is worth spending time to consider the political transformation of British India into the two successor states of India and Pakistan, since the way in which Britain finally relinquished her power and the courageous and magnanimous way in which India under Nehru forgave the bitterness of the preceding years and maintained the British connexion by staying in the Commonwealth guaranteed the modern multiracial association that we now have and influenced decisively the subsequent course of Commonwealth history.

Economically the independence of British India had other consequences. The old trade pattern continued with Britain retaining her position as by far the largest outside investor on the Indian sub-continent. But internally, faced with the poverty and backwardness of her vast population, India, which at Independence had a highly efficient, imaginative and adequate Civil Service, turned her attention to gigantic Five Year Development Plans. This decision, perhaps more than any other, really launched the economic process that in a few years led the rich nations of the West into accepting a major and long-term responsibility for aid to developing countries.

During the war Britain financed a great portion of her Far East campaigns by purchasing necessary supplies on credit in India. As a result India had piled up a huge sterling surplus in London. After Independence she began to draw upon her sterling credits in order to finance her ambitious development plans; in a few years, 1947–51, she had used the greater part of them and then faced either bankruptcy or the painful political decision of curtailing her plans. Despite her choice—unwelcome in the West—to be politically non-aligned in the Cold War struggle, she was now the world's largest democracy and strategically and economically so vital that, faced with the possibility of her economic collapse or of an internal revolution—if not communist, certainly communist inspired—the West embarked upon a major programme of economic aid that has continued ever since.

In immediate economic terms India's withdrawal of her sterling balances coincided with Britain's worst years of post-war economic difficulties, and it says a good deal for Britain's approach to her newest and largest Commonwealth partner that she never balked at losing so rapidly reserves whose continued 'banking' in London would have gone a long way towards easing her own problems. In later years Britain's ability and willingness to provide aid for India has acted as an index of Commonwealth economic prosperity and the degree of co-operation that has been achieved.

By 1948 the old white Commonwealth of five had grown to eight and its three Asian members had altered its whole character. In the same year Britain withdrew from Palestine. Irrevocably now the process of decolonization had begun, and although another nine years were to pass before further colonies achieved independence it was a time for rethinking some of the old concepts that had governed the Empire. In Africa and elsewhere serious attention had to be paid— and in some cases, regrettably, it was for the first time—to detailed plans for training the successors to the colonial authorities. The long-held economic criterion for colonies—that they must pay their own way out of their revenues (a rule that had been held to rigidly and only been broken in exceptional crises)—now came under scrutiny. With the advent of large-scale aid programmes it was inevitable this should happen; it foreshadowed new departures in terms of Commonwealth economic activities. Instead of the old policy the rich Commonwealth members began to help their poorer partners. The new business of aid, it is true, was headed by the United States, the scale of whose assistance outmatched anything the Commonwealth could achieve, but, nonetheless, the coming of the 'aid age' brought with it a whole series of new Commonwealth economic relationships.

THE BEGINNINGS OF AID

Aid is now a commonplace of international politics: it is accepted as a normal part of the relationship existing between rich and poor countries while its merits, limitations, potentials and misuse are constantly paraded according to the political needs of the moment. Yet the growth of aid programmes and the acceptance of them as an everyday part of diplomatic activity between countries is a very recent occurrence. Whatever the motives for aid giving—and they are many and varied—this is the first age in history when large transfers of resources from rich to poor countries have taken place at any rate in part for altruistic or humanitarian reasons.

American Lend-Lease to Britain in the war could be classified as aid; rather it comes under an older tradition—Pitt keeping Britain's European allies going against Napoleon by liberal supplies of gold. Moreover, the Americans were helping a fundamentally rich and technologically advanced country over a temporary crisis; they knew the money would be repaid. Again, Marshall Aid falls into a category of its own: its generosity is unquestioned but it was, once more, a matter of helping basically sound and modern economies overcome a crisis: a massive one-'shot' effort crammed into a relatively short period.

But the concept of a continuing flow of resources, year after year, to countries whose economies vary between extremes of weak and almost totally undeveloped to potentially strong and partially developed needing maybe ten years or so of assistance to bring them to the so-called point of economic take-off is something quite different. Much of the impetus for aid derives originally from the stresses of the Cold War. In the early years of confrontation between East and West it was assumed, often with an ingenuousness bordering on total naïvety, that weak and economically backward countries could be 'bought' into the Western or Eastern alliance systems by suitable offers of aid. Political realities soon dispelled that notion, though not before the failure of non-aligned countries to alter their political allegiances in gratitude for help received had caused considerable ill-feelings on the part of aid donors. More realistically much early aid was given to bolster the régimes of countries already friendly to one or other side in the Cold War. This is particularly true of American aid to Formosa or South Korea. Later, however, and conforming more obviously with political facts aid came to be given without any expectation of change in the alignments of the recipients; only in the hope that it would help to produce internal stability and economic progress.

Once she had overcome her own most severe economic difficulties—indeed during them—Britain rapidly developed into one of the major aid donors. Most of her efforts have always been directed into the countries of the Commonwealth. With the growth of the aid concept any developing territory became a potential candidate for assistance: in effect this meant the rapid increase of British aid to her colonies prior to their independence; the custom of a parting aid gift when they did achieve independence; and their subsequent expectation of more aid as Commonwealth countries. The rich members of the Commonwealth—Canada, Australia and New Zealand—increasingly joined with Britain as aid donors and co-operation between the four in this field has been one of the most fruitful economically in recent Commonwealth history.

The early stages of inter-Commonwealth aid drew inevitably upon past imperial examples; indeed, a good deal of the whole pattern of aid giving can be traced to already existing practices of the British Empire. In order to gain a perspective of Commonwealth aid it is worth examining, briefly, first, Britain's approach to development problems in the colonies; second, the growth of the Colonial Development and Welfare Corporation; third, a specific (and much-publicized) scheme, the ill-fated 'groundnuts' project in East Africa; and, finally, the Colombo Plan. A good deal of the later Common-wealth approaches to aid, the methods employed and the expectations of results can be traced to these earlier British attempts to aid colonial development or to the success story of the Colombo Plan.

A normal requirement of imperial financial policy had been for colonies to meet their budgetary expenses out of recurrent revenues. Except in emergency situations or crises it was not expected that London would be called upon to supply finance even for running expenses, let alone development. Slowly, however, the pattern had been changing. Grants-in-aid to colonies were first made in 1878. But this was aid in a very special form: if, for whatever reason, a colony could not meet its normal current budget then it could apply for a grant-in-aid. No colony liked to do so since the Treasury then insisted upon a detailed scrutiny of the whole finances and budget before a grant was made, on the old principle that no money could be voted from the British taxpayer without Parliament exercising control. It is one of the early origins of the idea of aid with strings. The policy was negative: less a question of aid to get the colony out of trouble than Treasury control to see it did not get in further.

The first real step towards a more generous policy of financial assistance for the colonies was the Colonial Development Act of 1929. This established a regular fund which could receive up to £1 million a year, the money to be made available either as a grant or loan to colonial governments. The stated purpose of the act was to help in the development of agriculture or industry in a colony so as to promote commerce or industry in Britain. There has been a good deal of subsequent debate as to whether aiding the colony's develop-ment or promoting British commerce and industry was the more important intention of the Act: certainly this dual purpose reflected normal thinking of the time. Between 1929 and 1940 £8·8 million

D

was disbursed to the colonies by Britain under this act; almost all the money went to the development of capital projects of an economic nature: it was not used for purposes of social welfare. Gradually, however, the old imperial concept of colonies meeting all expenses out of their revenue was receding; instead there was growing up a greater emphasis upon the idea of trust and the consequent responsibility to develop colonies for their futures. Events encouraged this view.

Serious rioting in the West Indies during the later thirties led to the appointment of a West Indies Royal Commission in 1938. Its report recommended that money be made available in grant form for the West Indies to promote social welfare services—particularly education, health, slum clearance and housing—and it pointed out that the islands could not conceivably find the money for this out of their normal revenues; therefore, it said, Britain should. These recommendations became the basis for the Colonial Development and Welfare Act of 1940 which provided up to £5 million a year to be made available by grant or loan to any colony for schemes likely to promote development or the welfare of the people.

The Act was debated and passed by Parliament at the time of Dunkirk. The circumstances of the time were extraordinary. Britain did not dare do nothing and leave a situation of violent discontent for the German propaganda machine to use against her. It can be argued, not without justification, that, as has so often been the case in Empire and Commonwealth history, she only acted generously when extreme pressures forced her hand; or that there was a magnificent quality about the act (its propaganda value not being overlooked) which began a major colonial aid programme when Britain was so hard pressed in war: a gesture of faith in the future of the Empire at a time when it was so dangerously threatened. In fact, as usual, it represented a mixture of motives. But the Act did break entirely new ground: it established the principle of direct British financial responsibility for development and welfare in the colonies. By 1946 schemes to the value of £30 million had been approved and £10·4 million had already been spent.

In 1945 a new C.D. & W. Act was passed which provided £120 million for expenditure between 1946 and 1956; from 1946 to 1966 a total of £340 million was allocated under the Act. During the debate in 1945 it was made clear that other sources of funds for colonial development—colonial government borrowing, private investment, colonial sterling balances and so on—would also be made available. Thus, with this Act Britain both accepted a responsibility for aiding the development of its colonies—and the principle came in due course to be extended to independent Commonwealth countries—and embarked upon her modern aid programme. However, wartime aid was not a one-sided affair; if Britain undertook responsibility to assist financially in the development and welfare programmes of her colonies they in return were generous in providing financial aid to Britain's war effort: a total of over £24 million in gifts was made by the colonies to Britain during the war and double this amount in loans. The economic reciprocity was genuine and by the war's end the habit of aid had at least been established.

Many development programmes have ended in failure. Few have been more costly or spectacular than the East African groundnuts scheme. Briefly, the history of the scheme was as follows: after the war there was an acute shortage of oils and fats and Britain, on rations, was particularly affected by this. A proposal for large-scale land clearance and the planting of groundnuts to help meet the fats deficiency was put up to the British Labour Government. The government accepted the proposals and decided on a major colonial development project. Acting as the agent of the government the United Africa Company began the operation; later, in April 1948, the Overseas Food Corporation was established and took over responsibility. This is not the place to analyse why it went wrong— no pilot projects, inadequate investigation on the spot, ignoring obvious sources of local advice, the political determination to produce quick results, the desire to demonstrate the success of a vast government-run development scheme and so on—the fact is that between 1947 and 1950 some £36 million were spent in Tanganyika, enormous clearing operations were carried out, roads were built, a new port was constructed, huge amounts of machinery were imported into the country, considerable numbers of often highly unsuitable Britons were rushed into the colony, all in order to produce ground-nuts on a massive scale. Yet by 1950 the whole operation had to be written off and no groundnuts resulted.

At the end Tanganyika benefited to the extent of the new port at Mtwara, cleared land, houses and equipment that were subsequently put to other uses, a number of Africans who had received training in a variety of skills, the fact that some of the best Europeans employed in the project then remained and gave valuable service to the colony. But all this, at the highest estimation, was worth less than a third of the total expenditure.

The principles involved in the scheme are both instructive and important. Whatever may be said about the mismanagement that led to such a costly and total failure, the concept had a certain grandeur about it. Moreover, a principle that subsequently lapsed but has recently begun to reappear in discussions about aid, this was clearly meant to be a two-way affair, providing benefits to both Britain and Tanganyika. The British Government was prepared to put up large sums of money to finance the project, so bringing a whole series of assets to the colony and providing it with a new agricultural industry that would materially improve the economy; in return Tanganyika would be enabled to supply Britain with a commodity she badly required. The long-term result would be an increase in trade between the two countries, welcome to both. There are two views about the scheme: the first that, despite its failure, it represented a magnificent early aid effort by Britain—a major attempt to assist in the develop-ment of Tanganyika; the second view, more cynical and probably more accurate, that the main motive prompting the British Govern-ment was the desperate shortage of fats then prevailing (and the political pressures of frustrated housewives demanding more mar-garine) and the desire to develop a source of supply that would fulfil the British demand as well as being in a colony where it could be controlled. No doubt the truth lies between these two extremes. But it does illustrate the mixed motives of aid that have prevailed ever since. Subsequent approaches to development projects of this kind were far more wary. Apart from the inhibiting factor of so large a failure it is interesting to speculate why. One answer may be that where an aid development scheme could and clearly was intended to result in providing an urgent British need, then both the scale and urgency with which the operation was tackled were very great. And this in turn demonstrates one of the key principles of aid and economic co-operation: the degree to which Commonwealth countries do co-operate is directly proportional to the benefits that both see emerging from a particular operation. Although in this case Tanganyika as a colony was something of a passive partner the principle still holds good. Whatever else can be said about the groundnuts scheme, it did at least establish the practice of Britain undertaking major development projects in the colonies and led on to the later assumption of continuing responsibility to help after colonies achieved independence.

Here then in the story of C.D. & W. and the example of groundnuts can be seen the beginnings of aid in the Commonwealth, at least from Britain to the colonies. Two criteria emerge clearly: that a rich Commonwealth country (in this case Britain but soon to be the other wealthy Dominions as well) should accept responsibility for the economic development of the poorer territories; and that the more obvious and immediate the benefit for the aid donor is likely to be, so by that amount will the effort be the greater.

In the early post-war period, however, the idea of aid to an independent Commonwealth country had yet to emerge, for the old imperial principle—that the donor of aid must be in a position to control and direct the use of its money—still prevailed. Clearly such control could not be exercised in the case of an independent country. The Colombo Plan provided some of the solutions to this problem of aid between independent countries.

In 1950 the Commonwealth foreign ministers met at Colombo to discuss problems of mutual concern. The most significant and lasting result of the meeting was the Colombo Plan—a Commonwealth scheme to assist in the development problems of South and South-East Asia. Already by that year India, Pakistan and Ceylon, though they had achieved considerable success in their various development plans, had also come to realize the sheer size of the problems they faced: rapidly increasing populations in countries already too crowded; mass poverty; ignorance; and disease. Britain and the other Commonwealth countries, particularly Australia with its own vital interest in Asian stability, were perhaps more concerned with the possibility of communism making gains in the area than in development if assistance were not provided. The result was a plan that not only worked remarkably successfully but also provided some valuable lessons in co-operation.

The idea of the Colombo Plan was basically consultative. All the Asian countries concerned already had their own development plans and were tackling these in their own fashions. But they recognized the value of discussing their mutual problems and difficulties together and seeking ways in which they could provide each other with assistance, if only at an advisory level. The non-Asian members such as Britain, Canada and Australia recognized a joint interest in helping their Asian partners and were, in any case, major sources of likely aid for the Colombo countries.

The Colombo Plan provided assistance in two ways: it acted as a clearing house or agent through which capital aid could be sought from outside by putting the individual members in touch with other countries, the World Bank or private sources of finance as appropriate; and it provided technical assistance in the form of technical experts or training. At this stage technical assistance was the main contribution of the non-Asian Commonwealth countries. Almost immediately the Plan was extended to non-Commonwealth countries—Burma, Indonesia, Indo-China in Asia—while the United States became an aid-contributing member.

The Colombo Plan itself never had large sums of money to use, nor did it enter into any detailed planning. It was always recognized that countries such as India and Pakistan would find most of the money to finance their development from their own resources; they would only turn outside to make up the gaps they could not meet. What was recognized at this early stage was the need for personnel with the special technical skills required to put their programmes into operation. The Colombo Plan became the channel through which the technologically advanced countries of the Commonwealth began to supply technical assistance to the Asian countries. In terms of the growth of aid the rich members of the Commonwealth contributed a considerable amount of technical help to their Asian partners before they became involved in large-scale financial aid by means of loans and grants. Even later only small sums of money were ever handled by the Colombo Plan.

The normal procedure of the Colombo Plan was to work out the particular needs of a member country and then put it into contact with the most likely source of assistance. Thereafter, once the two had been brought together, they would work out their own bilateral arrangements and the subsequent supply of experts or loan would receive the 'label' of the Colombo Plan.

The importance of the Plan, especially in the early 1950's, lay in two things: the joint recognition of a problem; and the method of consultation that was devised to meet it.

First, the recognition of the problem. When the rich members of the Commonwealth acknowledged that the problems of poverty and development faced by India, Pakistan and Ceylon (as well as other Asian countries) were also their concern they made an admission of historic importance about the whole relationship of rich and poor countries. Once this had been said it was only a matter of time before aid on an increasing scale was bound to flow from the one group of nations to the other. And whatever the reasons for this interest (see below, pages 99–105) in the development problems of their poorer Commonwealth partners, having admitted a concern they opened up a whole new phase of economic co-operation.

Second, the method of consultation devised. It has been claimed that the Colombo Plan rapidly took on all the 'club' characteristics of other Commonwealth bodies: informal meetings at the highest level which were not binding but rather a mutual discussion of problems followed by suggestions; then bringing together the appropriate parties—perhaps Ceylon and Britain or India and Canada—to see whether between them they could find a specific solution. The value of this informal approach has certainly been attested to ever since and, set against the tremendous difficulties of aid relationships between donor and recipient countries that have all too often

COMMONWEALTH 1966 -

Since this map was prepared Barbados
became the twenty-sixth independent
Commonwealth country.

·LLY INDEPENDENT MEMBERS

damaged the prospects of success in aid ventures, the Colombo Plan approach has clearly taught some valuable lessons in co-operation. In both Commonwealth and world aid-giving terms it has proved an outstanding success. The scale of operations, at least in financial terms, has been small when compared with other aid organizations; but the degree of harmony achieved in the extremely tricky process of negotiating assistance has been high. For the Commonwealth, the start of the Colombo Plan in 1950 signifies the real beginning of aid co-operation: the recognition by all that the development problems of the poorer members are a common concern; the need to consult closely and informally (something the Commonwealth was already used to doing); and the subsequent increasing flow of aid from the four rich and technologically advanced Commonwealth countries to the developing members of the association really begin in any co-ordinated sense from the inception of the Colombo Plan in 1950.

INDEPENDENCE

The year of independence for Ghana and Malaya, 1957 ushered in the last major phase of decolonization; ten years later only problems remained: the intransigent ones of Britain's own making such as Rhodesia; the little insoluble ones represented by the scattered collection of islands too small to stand as independent entities.

Both Malaya and Ghana were colonial territories of special economic importance. Between them from 1945 to 1957 they had been the biggest contributors of dollar and other hard currency earnings to the sterling area. Malaya as the world's largest tin producer (she also smelted her own as well as most of Thailand's) exported most of it to the United States, earning big dollar credits in return. In addition, as the producer of more than 30% of the world's natural rubber supply, her contribution to sterling balances was almost unique. The Gold Coast, producing more than a third of the world's cocoa, was the sterling area's other major earner of hard currency. By 1957 both had piled up large sterling credits in London; they were two of the area's most valuable members. When both became independent it was, apart from political reasons, a matter of considerable concern to London that they should remain in the sterling area. Both chose to do so and to become full members of the Commonwealth. Though habit is an important factor, they made their decisions for other reasons. Membership of the Commonwealth and sterling area had advantages for them in return for which they were quite prepared to keep their balances in London so that their achievement of independence did no financial harm to the structure of the Commonwealth.

Of equal and perhaps greater importance were the political results that followed. Commonwealth membership had now reached ten nations and the white countries were no longer in the majority. Instead it was five and five: Britain and the four original white Dominions; India, Pakistan, Ceylon, Malaya and the Gold Coast (now Ghana). Not only was the multiracial character of the Commonwealth beyond question but it had become clear that in only a few more years membership would consist of a majority of non-white nations.

As far as decolonization in Asia was concerned the independence of Malaya only left Britain with colonial responsibility for her Borneo territories and Hong Kong; the imperial chapter in the East was almost finished. In this respect Ghanaian independence was more significant. Not only was it the first British African territory to receive independence but the first of all the European black colonies south of the Sahara to do so. Up to that point the right wing 'imperial' element in Britain had, grudgingly, come to accept that the Asian Empire should become free and equal members of the Commonwealth association. They were far from ready to concede the same status to African colonies and a whole new process of re-educating a considerable segment of British society to a new phase of Commonwealth expansion had to begin. Furthermore, of the old Dominions South Africa had been sufficiently loathe to see Asian countries as its equals in Commonwealth councils; it was far more opposed to the idea of black African countries sitting at the conference table with it.

However, the plunge had been taken. The dynamic personality of Nkrumah, coupled with his fierce and effective advocacy of African freedom as well as his firm adherence to principles of non-alignment and opposition to any form of neo-colonialism (as he saw it), did much to ensure the rapid emergence of black Africa on the political stage during the next few years. Even so, with all the antagonism that Nkrumah roused in certain sections of the British public and despite his staunch and constant condemnations of every aspect of imperialism, he chose to keep Ghana in the Commonwealth. This example, especially in the light of Nkrumah's enormous prestige in Africa at the time, was of vital importance to the Commonwealth both economically and politically.

Thereafter events in Africa moved swiftly. In 1960 Nigeria, Britain's largest African colony, with an estimated population of between 40 and 50 million, very considerable economic potential (the discovery of oil in quantity a few years later made the promise far brighter), and offering a large potential market to Britain and other Commonwealth countries, became independent. British Somaliland also became independent that year but joined with Italian Somaliland to form Somalia outside the Commonwealth. Macmillan's 'Wind of Change' speech gave impetus to the process of decolonization. Meanwhile, France's colonies achieved independence under de Gaulle; so did the Congo, and the ensuing troubles there cast the one disturbing and frightening picture over an otherwise exciting year of progress.

But 1961 brought the inevitable crisis clash between South Africa and the other members of the Commonwealth. If it were to be a truly multiracial association the Commonwealth could not accept, even by the normal fiction of regarding South Africa's race relations as a purely internal matter, the Nationalist policy of apartheid: so South Africa left the Commonwealth. Thereafter in rapid succession Tanganyika, Uganda and Sierra Leone achieved independence.

Then the more complicated question of independence for Kenya and subsequently Central Africa—territories with significant white settler minorities—had to be faced. Despite the troubles of Mau Mau and the apparent intransigence of a considerable section of the white settlers in Kenya, the colony did become independent in 1963 and to the surprise of many made rapid progress in terms of racial harmony between black and white. In 1964 the Central African Federation was broken up, Northern Rhodesia later becoming independent as Zambia, Nyasaland as Malawi.

Despite misgivings about the pace and the tragic setbacks in the Congo, by 1966 all British colonies in Africa except for Rhodesia and the three High Commission territories* had become independent: all, except Somaliland, elected to stay in the Commonwealth. Now (mid-1966) the three High Commission territories are nearing independence; but the tragic and dangerous situation in Rhodesia, which declared UDI on 11 November 1965, has still not been resolved. How the Commonwealth develops in the future and particularly in Africa depends to an enormous extent upon what Britain eventually does in terms of discharging her responsibilities to the people of Rhodesia.

Outside Africa Cyprus, Jamaica, Trinidad, Malta and Guyana had also become full members of the Commonwealth by 1966.

Now in this rapid transformation of so many colonies into independent Commonwealth nations there emerged a number of new principles of great economic importance. In less than ten years from 1957 to 1966 the nature of the Commonwealth changed fundamentally: in the former year, even after Malaya and Ghana became independent there were still only ten Commonwealth countries, and even the smallest, Ghana, with a population of about 7 million, could claim viability as an independent economic unit. By 1966, however, with a Commonwealth membership of 23, one country had a population under 3 million, two had populations of less than 2 million, and five had populations of under 1 million. It is difficult if not impossible to claim genuine economic independence for units as small as Gambia and Malta; they frankly expect and Britain at least tacitly has agreed that she will continue indefinitely to support them with some form of development funds.

For long it was the stand of the British Government that economic viability—being able to stand on their own financially as well as

* Bechuanaland achieved independence as Botswana in September 1966; Basutoland achieved independence as Lesotho in October 1966.

politically—should be a condition of independence. But as the pressure from the smaller territories increased at the same time a-Britain's desire to disengage from her remaining colonial responsibilities, so was this principle of viability abandoned. The nearer Britain has got to her goal of total decolonization the more tortuously complicated the process has become. Independence for small colonies, some with populations of a quarter of a million or less, means long-term implications for both Britain and the other wealthy Commonwealth countries since a number of these little territories will not be able to stand on their own economically in the foreseeable future.

But economic co-operation implies a two-way arrangement with benefits to both parties. Where Britain or one of the other rich Commonwealth countries—Australia and New Zealand with their South Seas dependencies—is expected to bear an indefinite financial and development burden long after independence has been achieved, it may well be asked for how long the responsibility will be accepted. The hope is that it will: for sentimental and humanitarian reasons; sometimes for a specific return service or privilege such as a military base; and because it would seem a small enough price to pay at the ending of Empire.

There are still more than thirty small British territories to achieve independence. Some such as Aden and the High Commission territories will become fully independent between 1966 and 1970; others such as the smaller West Indian islands are to have special associated status, equal to full internal self-government and with a clause permitting them to claim independence at any time they wish;* the future of the remainder—mainly islands, including larger colonies such as Fiji and Mauritius and at the other extreme those such as Tristan da Cunha and St Helena with only a few hundred inhabitants—has yet to be decided.

The way Britain has attempted to solve the problems of some of the smaller and less viable colonies can be traced in part in the various stories of attempted Federations; Malta; the High Commission Territories. In all these instances economic considerations have played an important if not dominant part.

* Barbados achieved independence within the Commonwealth during November 1966

First, the Federations: Central Africa; the West Indies; Malaysia. The Central African and the West Indian attempts at federation both failed; that of Malaysia is still in the balance.

The fact that the Central African Federation ran into trouble almost at once is a classic illustration of the folly of subordinating political to economic considerations. The failure was political, because the Africans, especially in Northern Rhodesia and Nyasaland, did not (and rightly) trust the intentions of the white settlers in Rhodesia. Formed in 1953, the Federation boomed economically, but by the late 1950's political unrest was tearing it apart. All attempts to reconcile the African leaders in Northern Rhodesia and Nyasaland to the white politicians in Salisbury failed; and once the Monckton Commission had recommended that Nyasaland might secede the final break-up was only a matter of time. It came in January 1964.

The story of Central Africa illustrates perfectly how powerful economic pressures persuaded politicians to force a union of three territories in the teeth of all the evidence both as to the political intentions of the ruling white minority and of the political wishes of the black majority. At hardly any period of the Federation's ten-year history could it be claimed that racial trust existed between the two main groups. But powerful economic interests in Salisbury and London wanted Federation. Briefly and oversimplified it was argued that Southern Rhodesia with its large white settler element would supply the commercial and technical expertise as well as agricultural wealth in the production of tobacco; Northern Rhodesia would supply the capital from the Copper Mines; and between the two of them they would carry Nyasaland, which was poor and without sizeable resources except for its people, who would be a major source of labour.

Politically the white settlers saw Federation as a means of perpetuating or at least continuing for a long period their control of the area; and Whitehall was agreeable, partly for economic reasons—the concentration of British investment in the area is one of the highest in the world—and partly because it appeared to solve what had always been a difficult problem: meeting the wishes of a tough white settler group; while it would also provide a reasonable economic solution to the problems of Nyasaland. The experiment failed as it was bound to because it ignored the political wishes of the African majority.

Now in Commonwealth terms the three successor states each present distinctive economic problems. Rhodesia, in a state of rebellion, is involving Britain and the Commonwealth in sanctions; it is (whatever the eventual outcome) doing itself incalculable long-term damage, economic and political; and in the future the eventual solution of UDI may well be the most crucial turning point in the Commonwealth's history. By African standards Zambia is well off and its copper sales provide major sterling balances in London. Although UDI is doing considerable harm to the Zambian economy the long-term effect may be to make the country far more self-sufficient. Malawi is desperately poor and over-populated in terms of its resources. Federation may have been the right answer economically. As it is Britain has supported Malawi's annual budget since independence almost to the extent of 50% of its requirements and quite apart from aid to development.

Here then is one Commonwealth country that has to rely on Britain simply for its normal running expenses; there is little indication that this state of economic dependence will alter in the foreseeable future. Malawi must rely on outside assistance to survive and Britain has accepted the responsibility, but for how long is an open question. She tried to solve the question by putting Nyasaland into the Federation, but with its failure Britain must face the dilemma of a politically independent country which remains dependent upon her economic bounty.

The same situation exists in the West Indies. Federation seemed an obvious solution to the problems of the West Indies. Some of the smaller islands clearly could not stand as independent units either politically or economically. The difficulties, however, were considerable: distance, lack of communications, the markedly parochial nature of the different islands. Nonetheless integration seemed the most sensible course to follow. In 1947 a West Indies Conference held at Montego Bay accepted (apart from British Guiana) the principle of Federation. Even so, the members of the Federation were to have very wide individual powers, only assigning a restricted number of matters to the Federal authorities. Agreement to federate was signed in 1956; the Federal Constitution came into effect in 1958. In 1961, after holding a referendum, Jamaica withdrew; Trinidad, the only other island of reasonable size and some economic viability, followed Jamaica's example. Both sought and obtained independence within the Commonwealth a year later (1962) and the Federation had come to an end, leaving the small islands, the Little Seven, to try some federal arrangement of their own. Their future depends upon Britain's readiness to assist them with economic aid.

Now the breakdown of the West Indies Federation illustrates very clearly the extent to which Commonwealth economic co-operation is a practical possibility. In 1947 Jamaica was a very poor island and stood to gain as much as any of the others from federation; by 1960 its economic fortunes had changed: bauxite had been discovered and the bauxite and alumina industries had brought new wealth to the island; tourism and secondary industries had also prospered and Jamaica saw itself having to carry the weaker members of the Federation. It was not prepared to do so. In 1960, after discovering from Britain the conditions she required before the Federation could achieve independence—two of which were the beginnings of a workable customs union and freedom of movement between the islands—it appeared that Jamaica could then satisfy all the other requirements on her own. A 1961 referendum gave Bustamante a 54% vote against the Federation and for immediate independence. So Jamaica left the Federation.

Trinidad then had the choice (as the only other island that could reasonably stand alone) of trying to carry the Federation on her own—a difficult task that would have taxed her resources considerably—or following Jamaica's example. She chose the latter course. The point is that neither of these two islands, which alone in the West Indies had the size and resources needed for leadership of the Federation, were prepared to make more than an absolutely nominal economic or political sacrifice for the sake of the Federation, as a whole.

E

The Federation of Malaysia owed its inception less to economic considerations than to political ones: confrontation with Indonesia and a suitable way for Britain to hand over responsibility for its Borneo territories. There was a sound economic basis for it too. Malaya, Singapore, Sarawak and Sabah made a complementary economic unit though Brunei refused to join—with its oil revenues it saw no reason to do so: it could manage nicely on its own. So in 1963 Malaysia was formed; two years later in 1965 Singapore left and there is some doubt in the Borneo territories as to whether they wish to continue with the Federation.

Malaya forced Singapore to leave the Federation for political and racial reasons but with strong underlying economic motives. The commercial and entrepreneurial skill and thrust of the Chinese who form the bulk of Singapore's population have always given them a lead over the Malays, while the more rapid growth of the total Chinese population in Malaysia led the Malays to fear Chinese economic and then political domination. Once this had become apparent—and it did not take long after the Federation had been formed—the split soon followed.

In Malta and the three High Commission territories in South Africa Britain has been faced with small, economically weak territories for which some kind of graduation to independence had to be found. In the 1950's various proposals were advanced for Malta at a time when it was still considered to be too small (and too important for defence reasons) to stand on its own. The most controversial suggestion was that it should be integrated directly with Britain, sending M.P.s to Westminster but having its own home government in the same way as Northern Ireland. This came to nothing for several reasons, but not least because the precedent of such a solution would then have made it difficult for Britain to refuse similar links for her other island territories. Had many of them sought the same arrangement the whole character of the British Parliament would have been changed with a considerable influx of M.P.s all carrying equal voting rights and all representing areas with great economic problems that Britain would have been obliged to solve. Nothing came of this approach; the problems and the economic needs of the small territories remain.

The three High Commission territories—Bechuanaland, Basutoland and Swaziland—and especially the two latter which are dependent upon the goodwill of South Africa, have always presented particular difficulties. After years of financial neglect by Britain she has recently embarked upon a policy of hurrying them towards independence knowing this must inevitably throw them into the arms of a waiting South Africa. But it will relieve her of both a political and economic embarrassment that she appears only too willing to relinquish. Their eventual 'independence' or degree of subjection to South African policies will be determined by the amount of post-independence aid Britain is prepared to give them; the solution of UDI; and future British/South African relations. The outlook for them is hardly encouraging.

The final status of the small territories presents Britain with some of her most complicated problems and faces her with economic responsibilities that cannot simply be put aside: continuing the naval dockyards at Malta or finding an alternative means of assisting the island's economy; providing budgetary support indefinitely for Malawi—unless it can come to some customs or federal arrangement with its neighbours Zambia and Tanzania—and at present there is little prospect of this; undertaking long-term financial responsibility for at least part of the recurrent expenses as well as development plans in the small islands of the West Indies and elsewhere: these problems represent the economic left-overs of world-wide Empire.

In terms of modern Commonwealth co-operation, economic or otherwise, these small non-viable territories are Britain's responsibility first of all. Justifiably or not, a policy of maximum independence has been accepted even if it does mean a continuing need for financial aid after political independence has been granted. The most that can be hoped for in some of these cases is that the other rich members of the Commonwealth will accept with Britain some of the responsibility for aiding these territories. Here the picture of co-operation is an encouraging one. Long before Jamaica and Trinidad got independence Canada had undertaken an increasing responsibility for the

West Indies. She made clear her intention of continuing that policy. In the Pacific both Australia and New Zealand have shown considerable imagination in the way they have discharged their responsibilities towards small territories. It is to be hoped that in the future the richer members of the Commonwealth will continue to undertake economic obligations towards such weak units. No one else is likely to do so, and without help the territories in question face either absorption by stronger neighbours whether or not they desire it or precarious and poverty-stricken existences on the international 'bread-line'.

THE QUESTION OF BASES

The defence of the Empire led to the establishment of a series of bases at strategic points round the world. Decolonization and the changing status of British power, complicated by Cold War requirements, have made the whole question of military bases one of the most difficult and politically intractable that Britain has been obliged to deal with since 1945.

Withdrawal from Egypt led to the establishment of alternatives (or the build-up of already-existing bases) in Cyprus and Kenya. Independence in Kenya and the troubles in Cyprus, coupled with its doubtful military value, led to the abandonment of the Kenya base, the run-down of Cyprus (still going on) and the build-up of Aden. Projected independence for Aden in 1968, no matter what last moment agreements are made, means the base there will become obsolete or be de-activated not later than 1970 or 1971. A small British base or, rather, military presence remained in Nigeria after independence but was soon withdrawn, not for reasons of hostility between Britain and Nigeria but because British military presence there had become an embarrassment to the new government.

In only a few instances have bases been positively wanted: Malta opposed every British move to run down the naval dockyards at Valetta since at one time it was worth as much as £30 million a year in revenue. And so far, despite periodic pressures and political rumblings, the Singapore base (Britain's largest apart from the

BAOR in Germany) has remained reasonably welcome: first because of the war against the Communists in Malaya, then because of Indonesian confrontation. It too provides Singapore with an annual income which has reached £50 million in a good year.

Economically, few of the territories in which British bases have been sited could easily afford to dispense with them. And in practical terms it would appear to be a fair basis of co-operation to allow a base in return for the financial benefits accruing from the local military expenditure. But in fact, for political reasons—the desire to be non-aligned; fearing to appear to be a 'stooge' of imperialism; the need for a new nation to free itself of any imperial presence from the past—have all conspired to shorten the term that any military base has been allowed to remain in a Commonwealth country. Bases are usually unpopular whatever the economic benefits.

The history of British military bases illustrates certain facts about Commonwealth co-operation. The Commonwealth is not an alliance system; each member follows its own policy. Sometimes these coincide, sometimes they do not. The emotional nature of nationalism in newly independent countries ensures that the real or assumed advantages of a British base—whether economic, political or defence—are almost always overridden by considerations of freedom and anti-imperialism which, sooner or later, prove stronger than the proffered economic or defence advantages.

Bases represent a left-over of imperialism: for a time, therefore, because of particular local circumstances, strong British pressure, economic advantages or long-standing habit their presence is tolerated. But not for long. And this raises a crucial question about Commonwealth co-operation in all its aspects: to what extent is it simply a matter of hard-headed advantage either way; and how much is it the result of Empire, a continuance of habit that is almost bound to be a wasting asset?

CONCLUSION

A number of factors making for Commonwealth economic co-operation have been considered. So has the rapid process of political evolution that since 1945 has changed the old Commonwealth of the white Dominions and the British Empire into the quite different multiracial Commonwealth of today. The Commonwealth has many weaknesses; it is not difficult to criticize. Even so, there are very sound reasons for its continuation. Most important and least stated is the simple fact that, apart from Burma and Somaliland, every British colony on achieving independence has wanted to become a member. It makes no sense to assume they do so for reasons of sentiment or in order to pay a diplomatic compliment to Britain. Commonwealth countries are as tough and politically self-interested as any others. They stay in the Commonwealth because it is to their advantage to do so; when this is no longer the case they will leave.

It is not the purpose of this book to examine the various justifications for the Commonwealth, except in passing, though they will be looked at briefly at the end. Clearly, however, economic advantage is a major factor—if not the most important one—that holds the Commonwealth together. Since this is the case certain questions relating to economics have to be analysed without sentiment or false assumptions so that a valid judgement as to Commonwealth potential and the future possibility of its continuation can be made.

First, all the evidence of imperial and Commonwealth history demonstrates beyond argument that no country will enter into or long sustain economic arrangements that run counter to its own interests. No matter how strong the reasons for a continuing Commonwealth may be, if the price asked of individual members is such that they see themselves having to sacrifice their own economic advantage, then it is unlikely that the price will be paid.

Second, to what extent is the Commonwealth dependent upon habits left over from imperial days which are becoming, increasingly, wasting assets? This is particularly true in the economic sphere. The sterling area grew out of Britain's dominant position as a world trading nation; when the Empire evolved into the Commonwealth it was natural for members to remain in the sterling area. Yet Britain's sadly altered economic position in relation to the rest of the world has led to the progressive weakening of sterling until now it is at least in question whether it should be maintained as a world currency; while the advantage of belonging to the sterling area is no longer so apparent as in the past. Similarly, Commonwealth preference is a factor of diminishing importance in inter-Commonwealth trade; this again is a left-over from imperial days. The habit of looking to London as a source of finance—automatic in the days of Empire—is being steadily weakened because London often cannot meet Commonwealth needs when the United States can. The vast aid needs of the Commonwealth are more than 60% dependent upon non-Commonwealth sources of supply while the growing pull of alternate economic groupings—the Common Market, the United States, possible African customs unions—are becoming stronger.

None of this means that the Commonwealth does not possess real economic advantages for all its members; nor that these will not continue as factors in the Commonwealth's future. But the weakening of past links and the increasing attraction of outside influences draw attention to the need for a realistic appraisal of just how far Commonwealth economic co-operation is a matter of practical politics. If there is a future for the Commonwealth—and its potential role is immeasurable—then aims and priorities must be clearly understood.

Economics are no more than an instrument to be used in furthering other purposes. Thus, as long as Australia and New Zealand felt confident that Britain could defend them they did not look elsewhere; but when they realized she was no longer able to do so they did not hesitate to break the old pattern and conclude a mutual security treaty with the United States (ANZUS). Similarly, should a Commonwealth country feel that its economic interest lies outside the association it is unlikely to hesitate about breaking past patterns of economic co-operation.

In order to form an accurate picture of the strength and binding nature of Commonwealth economic links and co-operation the following must be considered: trade patterns, sterling and investment; alternative trading blocs; aid; neo-colonialism; immigration; future possibilities. Although it is often claimed that economic factors provide the only truly practical links the Commonwealth possesses it is the contention of this book that, granted they should be built upon and strengthened wherever possible, they are still only instruments; certainly in themselves they are not sufficient justification for the Commonwealth. That lies elsewhere.

CHAPTER 3

Trade, Sterling and Investment

WHEN either critics or defenders of the Commonwealth examine
the advantages that it offers to members or assess the value of its
so-called binding links, all put trade at the top of the list. Indeed,
many critics tend to dismiss as of little importance considerations of
common language and institutions, traditions of partnership and co-
operation or the varied methods of Commonwealth consultation,
often easier and far more informal than those operating between
other countries or in other groups. They may concede that links of
this nature are marginally useful and make for good relations; but
will then point out that only self-interest, not sentiment, will cement
an international partnership and, in terms of self-interest, trade is the
one obvious and major factor that makes the Commonwealth more
than a 'club' association.

There is considerable justification for this 'hard-headed' view
although it represents a gross oversimplification of both fact and
motive. Just because trade can be analysed statistically so that the
precise benefits are immediately apparent while other links can only
be judged in qualitative rather than quantitative terms does not mean
that these other factors do not have real importance. It is not possible,
for example, to measure the diplomatic and political value that taking
part in a Commonwealth Prime Ministers' Conference as an equal
with the other twenty-odd leaders has for the Prime Minister of a
newly independent and small nation: it is not just a question of
prestige but one of making an immediate series of contacts with
national leaders with whom he will later have to do business. Without
the Commonwealth connexion it would take several years to make
the acquaintance of so many heads of state. Politically, however,

there is great advantage in being able to say $X\%$ of our trade and $Y\%$ of our investment are Commonwealth, and consequently, that the association has this 'precise' monetary worth to our country.

Now there is no difficulty in demonstrating the extent and value of inter-Commonwealth trade; nor in arguing that the financial links of the Commonwealth—not just trade but sterling and investment as well—are obviously of the greatest importance to all its members. The questions that require answers are of a more complex character. Of course Commonwealth countries want to maintain any commercial or financial system that works to their advantage but it is relevant to ask whether these arrangements depend upon the existence of the Commonwealth; or whether the Commonwealth is held together because they exist. In other words, should the Commonwealth as an association be terminated, would this in fact make a great deal of difference either to the amount of trade that its members carry on with each other or to the way in which they continue economic co-operation?

There is a wide degree of Commonwealth economic co-operation, especially in the fields about to be discussed. Yet, since economics form so vital a part of any nation's activities, certain aspects of them—particularly trade—will not change with the alteration of a political relationship. Without the Commonwealth Britain would still want to buy Australian wool, New Zealand lamb, Indian tea, Ghanaian cocoa and so on; they in turn would still want to sell these commodities to her and take in exchange the machinery, cars, aeroplanes and other finished products she has to offer.

The fact that South Africa has left the Commonwealth has made no difference in practice to British–South African trade; if anything, its value has increased and so has the volume of British investment there despite general British disapproval of South African racial policies. And though the African countries condemn apartheid and have demanded a boycott of South African goods—and they have far stronger political and emotional motives for doing so than Britain—their trade to a large extent and with connivance at disguising trade returns still continues. Only an upheaval of major proportions such as a war, rather than a more negative state of no relations or the disintegration of a loose system of mutually convenient co-operation, is likely to make any fundamental difference to present patterns.

An assessment of co-operation in these fields, therefore, must be made with two considerations in mind. First, how far do the extent of Commonwealth trade, membership of the sterling area and investment positively act as binding Commonwealth links; and how far are they encouraged and increased by membership of the association? Second, to what extent would they fall away if the Commonwealth ceased to be?

THE PATTERN OF COMMONWEALTH TRADE

There is nothing intangible about Commonwealth trade: in both exports and imports it represents about a quarter of the total of world trade. A great proportion of this is between one Commonwealth country and another. Moreover, preference makes the Commonwealth the greatest system of trading discrimination in the world. As suppliers of primary products Commonwealth countries as a group stand even higher in terms of total world trade than when all kinds of goods are lumped together. Before looking at specific details, however, three general trends should be noted.

First, despite preferences, the trade arrangements between Commonwealth countries are loose and varied in nature: all are free to trade as they wish, to seek markets where they will and, in practice, preferences act as an incentive, often quite small, to follow an already existing pattern rather than providing the reason for doing so. Moreover, preferences vary enormously from one member or area to another: there is little uniformity about their application. Thus Britain only gives preferences on about 50% of her Commonwealth imports while the major West and East African countries give no preferences to Britain. Similar differences are to be found throughout the system.

Second, in the majority of cases, 50% or more of the trade of individual countries is directed outside the Commonwealth altogether. Sometimes neither Britain nor any other Commonwealth country is the most important market; in others the amount of trade with the United States or the Common Market is at least as great as with the Commonwealth. Where there is a good deal of trade between several Commonwealth members it is more likely to be the result of geography and obvious economic convenience than due to the Commonwealth connexion as such: thus, India, Pakistan and Ceylon or Australia and New Zealand are in any case natural trading partners.

Third, and most crucial to the whole question of Commonwealth trade is the position of Britain. To talk of Commonwealth trade as though it is a major exchange among the different Commonwealth countries would be meaningless if Britain were excluded. As the third largest trading nation in the world (after the United States and Germany) and as the great power most dependent upon trade simply to survive, Britain provides a huge market for Commonwealth products—especially their foodstuffs and raw materials—and manufactures a large proportion of the goods they require. In most cases, if British trade were subtracted from the total figures, the amount of trade between one Commonwealth country and all the others amounts to less than 25% of their total and this figure is often equalled or surpassed by the volume of their trade with the United States or the Common Market. The phrase 'Commonwealth trade' implies the amount that is carried on between them all and since the figures in some cases are as high as 70% (New Zealand) and in a good number around 50% it is natural to assume that the Commonwealth trade link is of major importance. When these figures are analysed, however, the picture alters dramatically.

Thus a country such as Ghana carries on approximately 30% of its trade within the Commonwealth; but subtract from this the figure for British–Ghanaian trade and then its total with all other Commonwealth countries falls to 7–8%. The same pattern recurs frequently. In other words, apart from Britain, the incidence of trade as between one Commonwealth country and another is not particularly high; often it is negligible. Consequently, to talk of the value of inter-Commonwealth trade to all its members is perhaps less accurate than to talk of the enormous importance of trade between Britain and each of her Commonwealth partners.

Once more this reflects old imperial patterns and suggests that Britain is the hub of the system. Trade was the spur to Empire and Britain fostered, as her interest dictated, a two-way traffic between herself and her colonies. This has continued naturally enough into the Commonwealth era. But whereas every kind of circumstance and incentive operated to encourage trade between Britain and her colonies, the same factors did not operate as between one colony and another. The historic reason for membership of the Commonwealth is that all were at one time in the British Empire. Until Imperial Preference was introduced at Ottawa in 1932 there was no special inducement for one Dominion or colony to trade with another and only where natural geographic or economic reasons existed had two or more countries of the Empire developed into major trading partners—as already mentioned between Australia and New Zealand or India, Pakistan and Ceylon; or, through imperial administrative convenience as well as geographic factors, as in British East Africa, did an appreciable amount occur.

Thus, in general terms, both the old Dominions and the colonies had established their trading patterns before the era of the modern Commonwealth; and if these, apart from Britain, were largely outside the Commonwealth framework, they have not altered much since.

The date 1956 is a useful one to examine: sufficiently long after the war that trading had resumed a more normal pattern than the artificially created one of tight sterling and quota controls; and before the Common Market had yet begun to exercise its subsequent power of attraction. In that year all Commonwealth and Empire countries (except Britain) exported 27% of their goods to Britain, 26% to the United States, 13% to the Common Market and 4% to Japan; they imported 23% of their requirements from Britain, 32% from the United States, 9% from the Common Market and 4% from Japan. At the same time the figures for inter-Commonwealth trade (less Britain) were exports 15%, imports 13%.

An analysis of these figures reveals that in terms of exports Commonwealth trade with Britain is almost twice what it is with the remainder of the Commonwealth; with the Common Market it is approximately half; with the United States about the same; while

Japan has become a serious contender for place. The picture with imports is not all that different: Commonwealth trade with Britain is lower but still much greater than with other Commonwealth countries; it is somewhat lower with the Common Market but considerably higher with the United States than with Britain. In other words, the United States was at least as important as a trading partner to individual Commonwealth countries as the rest of the Commonwealth, and vastly more so if their trade with Britain is excluded; Europe comes a substantial third on the list and was then increasing the volume of its trade with Commonwealth countries. However, there is one major distorting factor: Canada. After Britain, Canada is by far the largest and wealthiest trading nation in the Commonwealth and something like 70% of its trade is with the United States; consequently, when American–Canadian trade figures are subtracted from the statistics the United States' share of Commonwealth trade drops to approximately 10%.

Most of these trends continued or were accentuated during the ten years to 1966 and the total of inter-Commonwealth trade has remained proportionately about the same.

The importance attached to Commonwealth trade varies enormously from one member to another: for some it is vital, for most it is at least a major part of their trade, for Canada it is completely overshadowed by her trade with the United States. Approximately 30% of British trade is with the Commonwealth; yet it has remained static in recent years while that with the Common Market in particular has risen sharply. In terms of exports New Zealand, Nigeria, Rhodesia (before UDI), Sierra Leone and the West Indian islands were by far her best customers, taking 40% or more of their imports from her. For imports into Britain the pattern changes somewhat with Australia, Ghana and East Africa joining the others and selling her 40% or more of their exports. The economies of a few countries depend almost exclusively upon the British market: New Zealand, whose exports are broadly confined to meat and dairy products, has developed these for British consumption. If Britain substantially altered this trade the New Zealand economy would collapse: in this case both preference and the continuation of the present trade arrangements between the two are matters of survival for New Zealand. Similarly, in the West Indies, British Guiana, Jamaica and Trinidad have over the years found in Britain the one major market for their staple crop, sugar, and take by far the largest proportion of their imports from her; their second market is Canada. Not least of the reasons why the West Indian Federation failed was that all the islands had developed over the centuries a two-way trade between themselves and Britain, enlarged in varying degrees into a three-way trade to include Canada and the United States; but hardly ever had they developed more than nominal trade with each other. Thus, in theory, federation may have appeared sensible; in practice, certainly in trade terms, the existing links were tenuous and slight.

Analysing Commonwealth trade patterns in 1964 the broad picture was as follows: 28% of Britain's exports were to the Commonwealth and 30% of her imports were from it. Of other selected Commonwealth countries in most cases 50% or more of their total Commonwealth trade was with Britain.

In terms of exports only Pakistan and Malaysia of the countries quoted did not do more than half their total Commonwealth trade with Britain; in terms of imports only Ceylon, Malaysia, Zambia and Malawi did not do more than half with Britain but in some of these cases there are rather special reasons to account for the variation. Both Zambia and Malawi rely heavily for imports upon the more

COMMONWEALTH EXPORTS

Country	% Commonwealth trade	Britain's share
Canada	20	15
Australia	39	20
New Zealand	57	49
India	35	21
Pakistan	36	13
Ceylon	46	29
Ghana	20	15
Malaysia	37	12
Nigeria	42	36
Zambia	39	32
Malawi	70	48

Trade, Sterling and Investment

COMMONWEALTH IMPORTS

Country	% Commonwealth trade	Britain's share
Canada	13	8
Australia	41	27
New Zealand	69	38
India	22	14
Pakistan	21	13
Ceylon	37	16
Ghana	36	27
Malaysia	40	18
Nigeria	38	31
Zambia	61	17
Malawi	72	24

SOURCE: *Commonwealth Trade 1964*—Commonwealth Economic Committee

advanced economy of their neighbour Rhodesia (which in turn relied heavily upon Britain before UDI); Malaysia, possessing almost unique Commonwealth products of tin and rubber, has built up an export pattern that differs considerably from other Commonwealth countries with a far wider distribution especially to the more industrial Commonwealth countries, Canada and Australia; and, in recent years, to Hong Kong—no doubt for the China trade. Ceylon, although Britain is its biggest supplier, depends secondly upon its neighbour India, which is more developed industrially. Even if she does not have a 50% share, Britain is still almost always the largest Commonwealth customer for all the other members.

Of the smaller countries not quoted above—Sierra Leone, Gambia, the West Indies—if anything their trading patterns are even more dependent upon the Commonwealth as a whole and Britain in particular.

Commonwealth trade with the other main trading areas in 1964 was as follows: first exports—within the Commonwealth 32%, a drop from 37% in 1960; with the United States 21%, an increase from 20% in 1960; with the Common Market 15%, an increase from 14% in 1960 but down from 16% in 1963; of other groups it was 6% with EFTA (less Britain) and 5% with Japan. The pattern for imports was roughly similar: within the Commonwealth 30%, a drop from 33% in 1960; with the United States 25%, an increase from 23% in 1960; with the Common Market 13%, an increase from 12% in 1960; and for the others, EFTA (less Britain) 6%, Japan 4%.

Thus at present roughly 30% of Commonwealth trade is within the group, while of other trading areas the two major rivals are the United States with between 20% and 25% and the Common Market with between 12% and 15%. In general terms the Commonwealth still stands first while the United States comes a strong second and the Common Market third. However, if the trade with the United States and the Common Market is combined it then becomes more important than inter-Commonwealth trade as a whole. Even so, inter-Commonwealth trade continues to hold its own while trade with the Common Market has not advanced as fast as had been predicted a few years earlier.

Within the framework of the Commonwealth—although recently there have been a few marked increases in trade between Commonwealth countries other than Britain (Australia and New Zealand, for example) the system really depends upon Britain. Trading privileges, preferences and quotas may be extended variously throughout the Commonwealth, yet in most cases it is the bilateral trading arrangements between Britain and her partners that constitute the only real unifying factor. Moreover, British trade with Commonwealth countries is slowly but steadily declining as a proportion of her total trade. In 1925 Empire trade with Britain represented 38% of her total, while a peak of trading co-operation was reached in the years immediately after the Second World War when the dollar shortage and exchange control were in full operation. In subsequent years a series of factors: increasing convertibility, world pressures for greater free trade, lessening trade restrictions, the development of new industrial and production patterns, not only in the old Dominions but also in India and the developing members of the Commonwealth, the sources and patterns of aid giving, the emergence of the Common Market and other potentially important trade groupings—all these have led to a wider diversification of trade, often at the expense of inter-Commonwealth trade.

F

Most of these changes reflect general trends in world trade and the Commonwealth as a group and individually has had to take them into account. Even so, trade with their Commonwealth partners still remains the greatest single amount for most Commonwealth countries. But, to revert to an earlier question: is inter-Commonwealth trade part of the normal world pattern and not really dependent upon the Commonwealth connexion; or is it artificially stimulated because they belong to the Commonwealth? The answer can be found at least in part by examining the effectiveness of imperial preference. It is true that preference is quickly defended by Commonwealth countries and sometimes bitterly attacked from outside, yet its real value is probably overrated.

In the first place there has been a steady erosion of preference over the years since the 1932 Ottawa Agreements: the 1938 Anglo-American trade agreement abolished preference on Commonwealth wheat; the number of British exports receiving Commonwealth preferences declined from about 55% to 50% between 1937 and 1948 and this represents the war and immediate post-war period of greatest Commonwealth and Empire solidarity; the process continues with the value of preferences dropping from as much as 20% to as little as 5% in certain cases. In 1957 and 1958 Australia and New Zealand respectively came to agreements with Britain permitting them to reduce preferences they had arranged at Ottawa; in 1966 Zambia decided to end all preferences for Britain.

Reasons for these changes are numerous and often confusing. Thus preferences considered vital by Australia ten or fifteen years ago so as to give the products of its manufacturing industries a chance in the British market have become less important as those industries have developed. Canadian preferences offered to certain British goods of a high 'Quality' nature have had little influence upon sales since no other country has produced comparable goods. In terms of the British market some Commonwealth countries get preferences on 75% of their sales, some on less than 50%, some on less than 30%.

It is virtually impossible to say how much these various preferences influence the direction of trade. Of course, they make it more attractive but that is not the same thing. Some preferences are large enough to raise the volume of trade between Commonwealth countries while others do no more than make the position for an exporter easier and more assured within a particular market. It is doubtful whether preference significantly alters the flow of trade; rather, it helps to ensure that existing trends are maintained. The value of preference is more political. A change of trading habits involving the preference system will entitle a Commonwealth country's partners to consult with it first; while the existence and maintenance of preferences is advanced as a powerful reason for Commonwealth solidarity— they must be maintained, it is argued, or the Commonwealth will be weakened.

Apart from preference, commodity agreements are the most important Commonwealth trade links. Thus, Britain has guaranteed New Zealand free access to its market for meat and dairy products, guaranteed a minimum price for Australian meat and agreed to buy certain quantities of its wheat and flour. But the most effective of all such agreements, particularly as it assists some of the smallest and weakest economic units in the Commonwealth, is the Commonwealth Sugar Agreement whereby Britain has undertaken to buy fixed quantities of sugar at higher than world prices.

A brief general summary of Commonwealth trade patterns gives the following approximate picture. First, inter-Commonwealth trade at present runs at about 30% of the total of all Commonwealth trade and in most cases 50% or more of this is a two-way exchange between Britain and individual Commonwealth countries. Second, the United States with between 20% and 25% and the Common Market with between 12% and 15% are the next two trade partners of the Commonwealth as a whole and over the years have made steady gains at the expense of inter-Commonwealth trade. Third, that preference is probably more important as a factor in maintaining existing trends than in causing any re-direction of trade and is declining in importance although politically it represents a valuable Commonwealth bond. Fourth, in regional terms, the Commonwealth picture is as follows: Canada is overwhelmingly part of the American market with something like 70% of its trade with the United States and only 20% with the Commonwealth—this is unlikely to change; Australia and New Zealand, apart from heavy dependence upon the British market, are appreciably increasing their trade with one another; similarly, again for geographic reasons, India, Pakistan and Ceylon form natural trading partners; in West Africa there is an overwhelming trend towards two-way trade with Britain—for Nigeria 36% of its exports and 31% of its imports are with Britain as opposed to a total of 42% and 38% with the Commonwealth as a whole; for Ghana the comparable figures are 15% and 27% as opposed to Commonwealth totals of 20% and 36%; while for Sierra Leone the dependence upon Britain is much greater. In East Africa, apart from trade with Britain, Kenya, Uganda and Tanzania make natural trading partners and the volume of trade between the three in many respects now exceeds that between any one of them and Britain. The Central African picture is inevitably confused by UDI; but in normal conditions Zambia, Malawi and Rhodesia are obvious trading partners and even with UDI Zambia has needed to import roughly 35% of its total outside requirements from Rhodesia (double the amount from Britain). As for the West Indies and Guyana, their trade is basically to Britain, then to Canada, while the small amount of inter-island trade worked against the possibility of federation.

Commonwealth trade has grown up as the result of Empire; consequently the normal pattern is of trade from Britain to each Commonwealth country and back. Gradual changes are taking place both on a regional basis within the Commonwealth and between Commonwealth countries and industrial areas such as Japan or the Common Market. Most of these developments are the result of normal economic processes and only a few can be classified as highly artificial in the sense of a narrow confinement of trading partners—such as Britain and the West Indies or Britain and New Zealand. But whatever the reasons, Commonwealth trading patterns now exist after a particular fashion. All, in common with world trends, are trying to diversify. The Commonwealth connexion—whether the political fact of certain close ties and accepted practices or the economic ties of preferences and quotas—undoubtedly helps to maintain the present pattern and, in turn, the pattern encourages the continuation of the Commonwealth. However, it is highly probable that the greater part of existing Commonwealth trade would continue much as it is, though subject to swifter change, with or without preferences and whether or not the Commonwealth were there.

STERLING AND THE STERLING AREA

There are three international currencies—gold, dollars and sterling —and at present about 50% of the world's business is transacted in sterling. As a statement of fact that should be sufficient justification for the continuation of both sterling as a world-wide currency and of the sterling area. Unfortunately sheer size—the number of countries which belong to the sterling area, or the volume of business that is handled in sterling—does not of itself guarantee that the pound is either a strong currency in relation to the dollar or gold; or that it is necessarily suitable any longer as an international means of exchange.

We have already traced the reasons for the growth of sterling as a world currency and the formation of the sterling area (see above, pages 17–19); moreover, the particular difficulties that Britain and sterling had to face between 1945 and devaluation in 1949 can be ascribed mainly to the results of the Second World War. Not entirely, however; another reason was that commendably, perhaps, but not necessarily correctly in economic terms, Britain determined to remain a great power in a world sense and this political decision meant inevitably that she had to maintain sterling as an international currency. The burden of doing this fell upon Britain rather than upon the other members of the sterling area and so she had to compete first with the United States and then with the Common Market in order to do this.

Sterling crises have become a commonplace of British economic life ever since the war. The first such crisis came in 1947 after the attempt to make the pound convertible. Further troubles in 1949 and the need for deflation brought a second crisis and the devaluation of the pound. Whatever the economic effects of devaluation, and on the whole the measure was a failure, it did considerable damage to the prestige of sterling as a world currency. Moreover, since there was no consultation between Britain and other members of the sterling area before the measure was taken the British Government laid itself open to severe criticism from Commonwealth countries, who were subsequently forced to devalue as well. The Korean war in 1950 produced many of the conditions leading to the third sterling crisis in 1951; over-importing of primary products in sterling countries and inflation in Britain led to speculation against the pound. But in that year there was a change of government in Britain: the Tories returned to power and reverted to orthodox economic measures such as manipulating the bank rate that had not been employed since before the war. For the first time in 1953 there was no biennial financial crisis and optimists began to think the crises no more than a pheno-menon of the immediate post-war years; in any case, by then Britain was economically far stronger. But once more 1954/55 saw a crisis develop: it was controlled by drastic cuts in capital investment. Then came 'Suez' in the autumn of 1956 and renewed speculation against the pound; crisis followed and by 1957 it had developed into the most severe since 1947. British action in mobilizing her dollar re-serves from the International Monetary Fund, and her American Securities defeated speculators against the pound which once more gained strength. There followed four good years for Britain, helped by a dollar crisis in the United States during 1958/59 and steady European growth in the Common Market which was reflected in British and Commonwealth trade.

Monotonously, however, 1961 brought another crisis that was countered by a credit squeeze which in turn led to an almost stagnant British economy until it began to pick up in 1963. Still another crisis in 1964 was due to a larger than usual trade deficit (about £400 million) and a comparable movement of investment capital out of the sterling area. A new Labour Government came to power in this year and inherited the crisis. Instead of applying the kind of economic measures the Tories had adopted during the 1950's and early 1960's, what had come to be known as the 'stop–go' policy of deflationary and inflationary measures, they imposed a 15% levy on imports and introduced export incentives. These worked in part but by 1966 yet another crisis appeared: this time the government reverted to extreme deflationary measures, including a wage and price freeze.

Now all this—1947, 1949, 1951, 1954, 1957, 1961, 1964 and again 1966—makes a gloomy picture. Economists constantly debate causes and remedies. Is the attempt to maintain sterling as a world currency a mistake in view of Britain's relative economic weakness when compared with the United States and Europe? How big a difference does the fact that the trade of so many Commonwealth countries depends upon raw materials (commodities such as copper, cocoa and sugar which are notoriously subject to price fluctuations) make? How much are these crises the result of British balance of payments difficulties because, in keeping with the major world role she wishes to play, she maintains expensive military establishments round the world, gives considerable sums of money in aid to developing countries and pursues a policy of large-scale overseas investment? No clear answers have yet been found; but it is obvious that the fortunes of the sterling area rise and fall according to the economic position of Britain. To what extent, therefore, is membership of the sterling area an advantage to Commonwealth countries?

The first most obvious answer is that all (Canada never) have stayed in it after achieving independence. No doubt this is partly from habit: they already belonged as colonies. Still more it is for reasons of advantage. Just as Britain's colonies have not become members of the Commonwealth for purely sentimental reasons, neither do they elect to remain in the sterling area to please Britain. In nothing have Commonwealth countries been quicker to pursue self-interest than in matters of economics, and if membership of the sterling area worked against their interests they would leave it at once. In fact it does not.

What it offers are substantial benefits: prestige; membership of a long-established and loosely knit financial organization that does not attempt rigid control of individual countries; easier access to the London capital market; and augmented chances of aid and financial assistance in hard times.

Despite all the crises and fluctuations in sterling it still finances half the world's trade and so far it has remained 'safe' to belong. Though Britain's readiness to release Indian sterling balances during the late 1940's, a time of financial strain for her, appeared generous,

ECONOMIC ARE

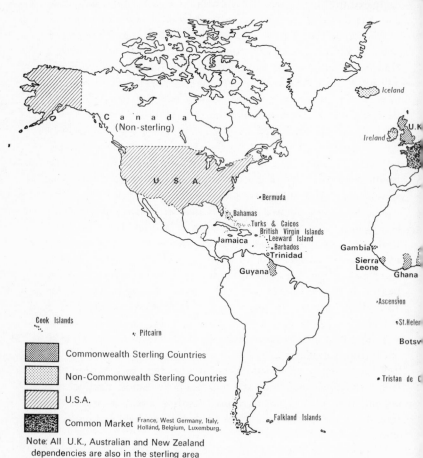

Iceland

Canada
(Non-sterling)

U.K

Ireland

U.S.A.

• Bermuda

Bahamas
Turks & Caicos
British Virgin Islands
Leeward Island
Jamaica
Barbados
Trinidad

Gambia
Sierra
Leone
Ghana

Guyana

•Ascension

Cook Islands

• Pitcairn

•St.Helen

Botsw

Commonwealth Sterling Countries

Non-Commonwealth Sterling Countries

U.S.A.

Common Market   France, West Germany, Italy,
Holland, Belgium, Luxemburg.

• Tristan de C

∘∘ Falkland Islands

Note: All U.K., Australian and New Zealand
dependencies are also in the sterling area

TERLING, E.E.C., U.S.A.

it was also essential. Had she refused to do so confidence in the
pound would have slumped permanently. And though members of
the sterling area may have been asked from time to time not to draw
upon their balances in order to help London, Britain has never
blocked their currency against their wishes. Even with its troubles
sterling remains the only rival to the dollar as a world currency—it
handles more business than the dollar; and if a Commonwealth
country decides to leave the sterling area what alternatives remain to
it ? Either to join the dollar area, assuming it is economically practical
to do so as well as being desired politically; or to stand alone in terms
of their own currency. For political if not economic reasons, few
Commonwealth countries would wish to tie their currencies to the
dollar; while standing alone has no obvious advantages and would
simply entail losing the benefits of sterling membership.

The loose nature of the controls within the sterling area are themselves an attraction. Most Commonwealth countries have established
their own central banks, mainly for prestige reasons but also to safeguard against a possible time when they may wish to leave the sterling
area. Increasingly, although they still keep the bulk of their balances
in London, Commonwealth countries are beginning to maintain
small reserves in their own banks. In 1966 both Malaysia and Zambia
started policies of converting part of their reserves into gold and
dollars rather than sterling. Their reasons are not entirely clear
though Zambia has to have dollars for trade with Rhodesia as long
as British sanctions are in force because of UDI. In both cases this
may herald a beginning of a move out of sterling. Thus, the establishment of central banks in Commonwealth countries and the holding
of at least a proportion of their balances by them rather than in
London does indicate a weakening of Britain's dominance of the area.

Probably the greatest advantage membership of sterling offers is in
terms of capital. After the United States Britain is by far the largest
overseas investor in the world and much of this investment is in the
Commonwealth. The willingness of British business to invest abroad
(sometimes encouraged, often deterred by British governments) has
provided a major source of capital to Commonwealth countries, and

the fact that the movement of capital from Britain to a sterling country is easier than outside the sterling area, especially during the frequent British periods of financial crisis, means that Commonwealth countries can usually find a good deal of the capital they require in London.

Secondly, for largely political reasons, Britain regards maintaining the Commonwealth as a vital aspect of its policy; in consequence most of its aid goes to the Commonwealth. The developing members who need aid therefore have a strong reason for remaining in both the Commonwealth and the sterling area. Furthermore, for a number of non-economic reasons, most members of the Commonwealth wish the organization to continue and prosper. The maintenance of the sterling area clearly assists in this, and if there are no strong contrary economic arguments they are quite willing to bolster the Commonwealth by staying members of the sterling area.

However, when Britain is in financial difficulties this affects the whole sterling area and other Commonwealth countries may well ask why their reserves should constantly act as a bulwark for Britain or be threatened when one of her crises becomes too severe. The answer is partly that although the rest of the sterling area helps 'rescue' Britain when she is in trouble, on the other hand, when her economy is doing well she in turn gives a major boost to the commodity sales of her Commonwealth partners and provides the investment capital they seek.

Even though sterling may be weak when compared with the dollar and the hard currencies of the Common Market there are no obvious alternatives, as the ready support supplied by both Washington and the European central bankers in times of crisis proves: it is not in either of their interests to see sterling crash.

Thus, allowing for all its weaknesses, sterling area membership offers more advantages than disadvantages and provides an important technical link that helps bind the Commonwealth together. If the past search for their own economic advantage by members of the Commonwealth is any criterion, none would remain in the sterling area if they did not consider it to be of real value to them.

INVESTMENT

British overseas investments are enormous: in 1966, though no exact figures are available, her overseas assets of all kinds—private investment in industry, oil and insurance, government investments and portfolio accounts—reach a total value somewhere in the region of £11,000–12,000 million. Only the United States has larger overseas holdings.

Traditionally, long before the sterling area came into existence, London had established itself as the world's major exporter of capital: throughout the nineteenth century Britain not only provided development funds for her Empire but also for the United States and Latin America. In the last years before the First World War her overseas assets had almost reached the then astronomical figure of £4000 million; even so, slightly over half this investment was in foreign countries, slightly less than half in the Empire. After the Second World War, despite having been forced to sell many of her overseas assets and incurring vast foreign debts Britain still had £2417 million invested overseas in 1945. During the twenty years since then she has pursued a steady policy of overseas investment until her present assets are greater than ever. She has more than recouped the war losses, and overseas private investment alone is now in the region of £6000 million.

The Commonwealth and the sterling area have always looked to Britain for capital: the fact that she has been able to provide it has been one of the great justifications (in Commonwealth terms) for the sterling area. Despite the lean years after the war Britain did soon regain her ability to invest overseas, and though far from able to meet all the demands that were made upon her she still maintained a high outward capital flow. From 1958 to 1966 the annual average figure for private investment throughout the world stood at £250 million—in 1964 it reached a peak of £371 million—much of this representing profits from already existing investments that were ploughed back.

But Commonwealth capital needs have far outstripped British resources. Thus Australia which previously looked only to London has in recent years experienced a drastic change in its investment pattern. In 1945 capital investment from outside in Australia was negligible when compared with British holdings. Every year since the war, however, 90% of the capital flow into Australia has come from Britain and North America, but whereas in the 1940's the United States was only involved on a small scale, by the 1950's American investment was increasing rapidly. In 1953 64% of the flow of overseas investment into Australia was British, 25% was American; by 1964 the figures were 45% each. This change reflects the more general picture in the Commonwealth as a whole, although hardly to such a marked degree: the steady and increasing replacement of, or at any rate partnership with, Britain by the United States as at least an equal source of capital to Commonwealth countries. In the Australian case the change also mirrors trade trends: in 1953 when American investment there was only 25% of the annual flow her share of Australian trade was 11% and Britain's 49%; but in 1964 when her investment equalled that of Britain at 45% of the annual flow her share of Australian trade had risen to 23%, Britain's had dropped to 28%.

Canada has always been outside the sterling area and tied to the dollar; her economy is bound far more closely to that of America than Britain or the Commonwealth and geographically and economically this has been inevitable. American capital investment in Canada is so vast that periodically it sparks off Canadian debates about their status as an American economic satellite; it is variously reckoned that between 60% and 75% of Canadian industry is controlled from the United States. Canada therefore tends to welcome any investment that helps offset so great a dependence upon one source, and the British stake in Canada—second to that of the United States by a very long way—is nonetheless substantial. In 1963 private investment not including oil and insurance stood at £326 million, and with portfolio and government holdings is very much greater, possibly £1200 million.

In other Commonwealth countries Britain remains the primary outside source of capital. Her stake in Nigeria is over £300 million, her holdings in Central Africa are larger still while Kenya, Uganda and Tanzania depend mainly upon Britain as the source of capital.

In the case of India, British investment has maintained its lead over all other sources ever since independence.

Whereas in the past Britain was expected to provide the bulk if not all investment capital in the Commonwealth her position has now become that of a major supplier but one who is unable to meet anything like all their needs. Instead the United States has stepped into the gap to supplement, equal or surpass the rate of British investment, while the Common Market has also become a substantial source of investment funds and the rich Commonwealth countries are beginning to provide some of the capital that the developing members need.

Several factors in the Commonwealth investment pattern are worth attention.

1. As Britain's inability to meet their demands has increased Commonwealth countries have adopted measures to attract capital from other sources. One of the best examples of this can be seen in the policies of investment incentives—tax-free establishment periods and so on—which Jamaica and Trinidad have offered to United States and Canadian investors; they have had considerable success in attracting light industries from North America to settle in their territories.

2. As always, economic advantage—likely profits and an investment's long-term prospects—have been the first consideration with British business. The remarkably high rate of British overseas investment in the late 1950's and early 1960's has been directed as much outside the Commonwealth—to the United States, Europe, Latin America (though much less) and to the Middle East oil countries (sterling but not Commonwealth)—as to Commonwealth countries. In other words, had Britain put political considerations of building up the Commonwealth before those of economic self-interest she could well have met most if not all Commonwealth capital demands, though at the expense of more profitable investments elsewhere.

Thus in 1963 private business holdings overseas (apart from oil and insurance) were estimated as follows: the United States, £666 million; the Common Market, £145 million; other European countries, £66 million; Latin America, £105 million: a total of £982 million; Canada, £326 million and the sterling area (mainly Common-wealth) £1985 million. This pattern continues.

3. A new factor has recently come to inhibit British business investment in some of the developing Commonwealth countries and that is the fear of political instability and possible nationalization. To what extent the fear is justifiable it is impossible to say; nor can the effects be measured in terms of how far investment decisions are influenced by it. But Abadan, Indonesian take-overs, the Zanzibar revolution (as well as downright prejudice about new African governments) leads some sections of British business to argue that risks in new Commonwealth countries are too great—there are likely to be revolutions or nationalization or a refusal to allow profits to be repatriated; therefore they prefer 'safe' countries such as Australia or Europe. No doubt these fears are understandable, and it only requires one or two instances of developing countries taking over foreign assets (Abadan is still quoted) or political instability as in the Congo for business interests to become shy of any form of invest-ment. Yet there is little evidence that investment is in fact threatened in this way; the few examples that do exist—Cuba, Iran, Indonesia, Zanzibar—must be offset against the vast majority of new developing countries which have scrupulously honoured agreements with private business. No matter what the politics of new countries may be—usually socialist and often one-party systems as well—the fact is they need all the investment they can attract and few of their leaders are so blind or shortsighted as to take the kind of economic action that will frighten investment away.

Certainly, some political leaders have made little effort to quieten such fears: if they want private funds they should be prepared to offer inducements or guarantees against political interference. This does happen to an extent: apart from the example of the West Indies (already quoted above) other countries such as Uganda have adopted partnership techniques whereby an overseas firm will work with the government through the medium of the Development Corporation. But more than this is required. Whether fears of unrest or national-ization are justified does not matter; the point is they exist. It is not sufficient to deny the possibility of commerce being harmed in this fashion; it is also necessary positively to invite overseas investors by offering inducements for them to bring business into the country.

However, the political conservatism of many British businessmen engaged in overseas ventures is notorious. Partly due to such fears there has, for example, been a measure of British disinvestment from East Africa. And there is an increasing tendency for business to ask too much. When a country is considered to be a 'risk' business will only move in if it can get a high return on its capital, often as much as 30%. This may be fair enough and in the past would certainly have proved acceptable. But today, where a 'new' country is concerned, not only does business expect to get such high returns but it also asks for government guarantees against possible loss due to take-over or political trouble and tries to get the local government to guarantee it as well.

Business should not expect to have things both ways. If a country is a risk there is a justification in asking for high returns; if, however, they do get guarantees they ought to accept lower profits. Too many seem unprepared to do so. Mainly this is a question of political education. Despite all the turmoil and changes during the last few years in Africa, apart from the Congo and Zanzibar, business has been left alone and more often than not has flourished as well. It is a commentary on political attitudes—and British lack of under-standing of the African scene—that if an investment in Europe fails the failure is put down to normal business risk; but if the same kind of failure occurs in a new African country the chances are it will be ascribed to political causes.

No doubt this is a passing phase, but such attitudes demonstrate rigidity and prejudice in the approach of many business concerns while the demands for double safeguards—high profits and guaran-tees—show a sad lack of courage in a country whose whole fortunes have always depended upon a suitably adventurous commercial spirit.

In summary, Britain is still the main source of private investment capital (not aid) for the greater part of the Commonwealth, although the United States is now catching her up at least in some of the more 'safe' investment areas such as Australia. However, Britain cannot provide anything like the total of funds that Commonwealth countries seek and, apart from the United States, European countries are beginning to look seriously at Commonwealth investment possibilities. The rich Commonwealth countries are also providing some investment in the rest of the Commonwealth.

Commonwealth co-operation in the three spheres of trade, sterling and investment is very great indeed, certainly the most tangible of all Commonwealth links, and though these may have developed out of past imperial patterns and habit they continue for reasons of self-interest. As long as they see their advantage being served by these links Commonwealth countries will do nothing to weaken them. But if other trading and financial alternatives appear more attractive to them, then these will be turned to and adopted. Nothing illustrates the point more clearly than Commonwealth reactions to Britain's attempt to join the Common Market.

CHAPTER 4

Economic Blocs

MUCH argument has been advanced to show how often economic self-interest has come first with Commonwealth countries. If the somewhat nebulous values of the Commonwealth concept and the possibilities of greater strength deriving from actions designed to foster its unity have been balanced against an individual member's economic advantage, predictably, the latter and narrower interest has triumphed over the wider but less understood one. This is hardly surprising for the greatest Commonwealth failure to date has been the almost universal inability of its different leaders to recognize in it more than an association that might render to their particular country some specific and immediate advantage.

Thus, all pay lip service to it in general terms and praise the ideals embraced within the phrase 'multiracial', while in practice all search for quick and useful returns. When they believe benefits to be forthcoming Commonwealth leaders are loud with their praises; when difficulties arise or they do not get what they want out of the association the story becomes a very different one and failures lead to quick despair. Then the Commonwealth is ignored or decried while its opponents try to write it off altogether.

At the one extreme it is fashionable for British politicians to talk of the Commonwealth in glowing terms, especially at election times, regarding it as a useful instrument of Britain's foreign diplomacy; and then to become cynically disinterested when they discover that the other members have ideas of their own about world affairs and are not simply prepared to act at London's bidding. At the other extreme, leaders of certain African member nations show perhaps the best understanding of Commonwealth multiracial possibilities, yet when difficult issues arise are too quick with threats of secession unless Britain acts in the way they believe to be right. A middle group complain or praise as events dictate but without particular enthusiasm either way; the association does offer benefits—of trade, aid, diplomacy, perhaps defence—and they take what they can get, making their expected and usually minimal contributions to the Commonwealth in return.

These approaches are negative and selfish. The Commonwealth will not survive indefinitely if its members cannot see in it values of a more universal and positive nature than simply their own advantage or a weapon of diplomacy to be used as a lever against another member, usually Britain. It may be an accident of history that the association has evolved and that so disparate a group of nations—reflecting most of the world's extremes of wealth and poverty, most of its political systems and alignments, and most of its races, colours and religions—has developed a habit of close co-operation; but it will be a major tragedy that future history must surely condemn if its members, through blind pursuit of their own advantage only, fail to use the instrument of the Commonwealth to tackle jointly some of the wider and more urgent problems that face the world.

All nations seek advantages for themselves and powerful economic benefits will always override weak political ties. This much at least is plain from past Commonwealth history. More significant is the fact that, despite counter-attractions to the Commonwealth as well as the divisions that continually occur within its membership, it has survived at all: the shock over Britain's Suez adventure; the bitter and continuing quarrel over Kashmir between India and Pakistan; the unhappy failures of Commonwealth federations and Singapore's present isolation from Malaysia; the disruptive effects in Africa of Britain's weakness in dealing with Rhodesia's illegal declaration of independence—have all threatened but, as yet, none has succeeded in breaking the Commonwealth.

Now this may appear to be an unconnected and unusual approach to the question of blocs; in fact it is not. Whether or not a country remains a member of a group, deserts one to which it has previously belonged or seeks to join a new one is entirely a question of advantage. And though, for example, individual economic interests have constantly worked against more general considerations of Commonwealth unity this is not to say that economics are more important than politics. In the long run the contrary is normally the case. Economics appear to win when their benefits are immediate and obvious. But if there is a straight clash between politics and economics, political considerations will come first. The truth of this contention can be traced in the approach to economic blocs or groupings by Commonwealth countries.

Thus, for the sake of very great economic advantages, real or imagined, as opposed to the vague and less understood values of the Commonwealth (which at the time many people described as no more than sentimental) Britain was prepared to sacrifice the Commonwealth in order to get into the Common Market; yet the clear economic values of federation in Central and East Africa, in Malaysia and, to a lesser extent, the West Indies have either foundered or at present are precariously balanced on the edge of failure because they have conflicted with political considerations of race or nationalism.

The attraction of economic blocs for Commonwealth countries consists of two kinds: those of a massive and powerful nature whose pull is so considerable that it might draw a member out of the Commonwealth altogether; and smaller regional groupings that may be within the Commonwealth (federations) or embrace nations of a particular area whether Commonwealth or not. Of the first kind are the Common Market and the United States; of the second, regional trading blocs—a possible East and Central African trading union or common market—or the suggested 'Maphilindo' between Malaysia, Indonesia and the Philippines. The attractions of the former could disrupt the Commonwealth entirely; associations of the latter kind would be unlikely to do so.

The present world is dominated by the bloc concept: the Communist bloc; the West; the Common Market; the Afro-Asian bloc; the Alliance for Progress and Organization of American States; or, military alliance systems: NATO; the Warsaw Pact; SEATO;

CENTO; ANZUS; while even larger and at present vaguer possibilities—Pan-Africanism or an Atlantic Community—hover in the background. Of all groupings only the United Nations and the Commonwealth transcend the regional, defensive and ideological concepts of these more narrowly based blocs. At present world divisions are so acute and numerous that the United Nations is unlikely to achieve more than a holding operation for many years to come. The Commonwealth, on the other hand, starts with a basic advantage over the world organization: it was not established as an ideological answer to world problems but developed organically from an existing system—the Empire; while its membership is still sufficiently small that it possesses enough common grounds from which it might successfully evolve a single purpose. Whether this potential is recognized in time or not depends first upon the Commonwealth's ability to avoid disintegration because of internal divisions, and second upon its response to the challenge of counterattractions from outside.

Whatever may develop in the future, only two blocs—the Common Market and the United States (which for this purpose may be considered as a bloc)—at present offer sufficiently powerful political and economic attractions to disrupt the Commonwealth. In the case of the Common Market, British membership in fact if not in name could spell the end of the Commonwealth; in the case of the United States the sheer extent of its political and economic pull may be enough to attract into its orbit at least Canada and Australia, perhaps the West Indies. Of other regional groupings only African possibilities at present seem likely to alter Commonwealth alignments.

THE COMMON MARKET

In less than ten years, following its inception in 1957, the Common Market has developed into one of the most dynamic forces in the world. Out of post-war weakness and disunity Europe has re-emerged with the potential to rival both Russia and the United States. So far most emphasis has been placed upon the economic reasons for a united Europe; but, in fact, the political reasons behind the Common Market are more important. The history of the Common Market illustrates how easy it is for economic considerations to cloud political issues. And since members of the 'Six' wish to play down political motives, as well as being unready to face the psychological implications of political unity, the predominance of economic arguments has been welcomed and encouraged.

It is, however, absurd not to recognize the clear political nature of the Common Market. The motives that led to its formation were many and complicated; some were never stated explicitly at all; others have barely been recognized; but they exist. It is perfectly true that the idealism of such men as Monet and Spaak envisaged a united Europe free from the divisions that have plunged it into war so often over the centuries. They hoped to recreate the old dream of 'Christendom'—a Europe where cultures, politics and economics combined to make a single 'nation'. They had the political realism to approach their dream through the positive attractions of economic prosperity, and since the appeals of greater wealth depended upon closer cooperation it was not difficult to sell the idea of a united Europe by the concept of a common market. But right from the start political unity was the aim; and though genuine idealism, particularly among young Europeans, remains a vital and impressive factor, other more dubious 'power' motives are basic to the Common Market idea.

Briefly, the Common Market rests upon the following foundations: positively, it aims at greater European prosperity; integration and unity of its members; a peaceful solution of divisions and quarrels instead of recourse to war; an end to European nationalism, to be replaced eventually by common 'citizenship'. Negatively, the reasons behind it are more disturbing: fear of Germany and the consequent desire to create a supra-national body within which she could be contained and controlled; fear of Russia and an equal desire to make Europe strong enough to face her as an equal; resentment of American power and influence and the subsequent wish to make Europe sufficiently independent that it need no longer rely upon the United States; and, always unstated, resentment at the loss of Empire fostering a new kind of economic imperialism that sees Europe helping to guide the development of new countries and treating Africa as a natural 'hinterland' for economic exploitation.

The danger to the Common Market if such negative reasons become dominant is very great; instead of a supra-national Europe above the old nationalisms they threaten to produce a super-national Europe, one more giant world power equal to the United States and Russia. Should this come about there will merely have been reproduced on the world, super power scale, the precise conditions which in a former age led to the great European wars: huge powers uneasily facing each other and manoeuvring for position until growing tensions lead to war.

When the Common Market began Britain stood aloof; her pragmatic approach to politics makes her instinctively suspicious of such groupings and in this case she was almost certainly correct. Instead she tried to break down its close political nature by proposing a looser free trade area to embrace all western Europe. When this was rejected she formed EFTA or the 'Outer Seven' as an economic counter-measure. Her reasons for opposition were various: the Commonwealth, her world-wide interests, the special relationship with the United States—none of which were compatible with close integration into Europe. Unfortunately for this policy the Common Market prospered and Britain did not—to anything like the same extent. Moreover, a combined market of 200 million in Europe rapidly became a dangerous trade rival to Britain, while possible exclusion from so wealthy a market not only threatened British economic strength but the country's entire trading future.

Suddenly the benefits of membership became apparent and political pressure to join increased. Economic arguments for membership appeared very strong; the debate grew; and, as usual, attempting to have the best of several worlds at once Britain, applied to join the 'Six'. She tried to persuade Commonwealth countries (and herself) that joining Europe would not hurt them economically nor destroy the Commonwealth politically; but she made it clear that she intended to join anyway. After 18 months of intensive negotiations, however, de Gaulle broke off the discussions and Britain remained outside Europe.

Now this is not the place to argue at length over the merits or dangers of the Common Market. All that requires saying is that full British participation in the Common Market would be incompatible with a real effort to sustain the Commonwealth connexion. And though there have been a number of ineffectual attempts to argue that Britain could do both—become a full member of the Common Market and somehow not damage the Commonwealth in the process—few people have been persuaded such an arrangement could work. In fact it is a matter of choice and Britain must decide: the Commonwealth or Europe.

As so often proves the case, the tangible benefits of joining the Common Market appear more obvious than the less easily discernible advantages of putting the Commonwealth first. In Britain there are plenty of people who would prefer to see the country throw in its lot with Europe where, they say, it belongs than cling to the weaker Commonwealth association which they would describe as politically doubtful and nostalgically sentimental. That is not the argument of this book.

What should be clear by now is that after twenty years of indecision by Britain: behaving as a world power without the necessary resources; attempting to play an equally commanding role in three main spheres of activity—the Atlantic Alliance, Europe, the Commonwealth—when in fact she only has the strength to pursue one of these policies successfully, Britain must make up her mind what she wishes to do. This has yet to happen. When the Tories under Macmillan negotiated to get into Europe the Socialists in opposition were loud in their defence of the Commonwealth; by 1966 having returned to power the Socialists appear eager to join the Common Market. The point is of course that the Common Market exercises so powerful a pull that it is at least likely Britain will eventually surrender to its attraction and sacrifice the Commonwealth in the process. Apart from the advantages of joining Europe the question is whether Britain can afford to stay outside so powerful an economic and political union on her doorstep. Further, advocates of membership ask why Britain should put the Commonwealth first when its advantages are often hard to define; its unity only rarely apparent; and the nebulous nature of its future potential is hardly ever suggested, much less understood.

Now Britain's behaviour towards the Commonwealth during her negotiations to join the Common Market and the reactions of the Commonwealth countries were both highly expressive of their general attitudes.

After first ignoring and then trying to disrupt the Common Market by forming rival blocs Britain eventually applied for membership; she insisted, however, that she would only do so if suitable arrangements could be made to safeguard the trade of her Commonwealth partners. Throughout the negotiations both the Tory government and the Socialist opposition maintained their loyalty to the Commonwealth which, they said, must come first. Apart from the clear impossibility of Britain obtaining the sort of trading concessions for Commonwealth countries that represented the minimum necessary to avoid hurting their interests, it is difficult to believe in the sincerity of British protestations. As the negotiations continued through 1962 Britain abandoned one after another all the original conditions she had insisted were essential to safeguard her Commonwealth partners. In the end, before de Gaulle's veto, it had become increasingly clear that Britain would betray Commonwealth interests as the price of entry. As on so many previous occasions in imperial and Commonwealth history it was now Britain's turn to demonstrate that she considered her own economic advantage more important than less easily definable concepts of Commonwealth unity. Britain was behaving selfishly but it could at least be argued (as it was at the time) with considerable force that she had no choice. Events subsequently disproved this.

But if Britain was selfish and prepared to sacrifice her Commonwealth partners for what she considered to be her own greater interest, the rest of the Commonwealth hardly behaved less selfishly. Once it had become obvious that Britain was negotiating in earnest and was determined to get into Europe, Commonwealth protests came loud and fast. The nature of the protests was almost entirely selfish: each country demanded absolute protection of its own interests while few paid more than passing attention to Britain's genuine economic distress or the difficulties that the choice presented to her. The anti-British clamour that arose from her partners was concerned neither with the threat to the concept of the Commonwealth as a whole nor with the possible loss for the world that the disintegration of the Commonwealth would entail: they were entirely absorbed with individual fears of damage to their own economies. Occasionally, it is true, arguments about principle—that the Commonwealth was a unique multiracial experiment which had to be preserved even at sacrifice (in this case Britain's sacrifice)—were advanced, but usually because they added weight to the more practical ones about preferences and markets. It was not an edifying spectacle. Some of the more vociferously selfish attacks upon Britain came from the old Dominions while only Nehru of Commonwealth statesmen reflected more thoughtfully upon the retrograde aspects of Britain turning its back upon a hopeful multiracial experiment for immediate economic gain. In the end de Gaulle saved the Commonwealth and the danger passed for the time being.

In retrospect this Common Market episode demonstrated three things. First, that the political and economic strengths of the Common Market are so great that they almost caused Britain to turn her back on the Commonwealth and may yet do so in the future. Second, that Britain and most Commonwealth countries were almost entirely selfish in their approach to the whole problem. Britain being prepared to surrender one by one the interests of Commonwealth countries for her own advantage; Commonwealth countries treating Britain almost like a pariah because she dared put her own economic interests before theirs—something which few have ever hesitated to do themselves. Third, and most dangerous as well as sad, almost no Commonwealth leader opposed British action in the positive sense of saying why the Commonwealth has a value that is worth preserving even at sacrifice to its members. If in the future Britain does get into Europe this could yet spell the disintegration of the Commonwealth. Meanwhile, Nigeria has obtained associate status, the East African Commonwealth members are negotiating for it. In the wider European context British membership of EFTA is no threat to Commonwealth interests; nor is the association strong enough to be more than a very poor alternative to the Common Market.

THE UNITED STATES

The startling growth of American power during the Second World War and subsequent American domination of the whole Western world represent a major shift of the balance of power. No country has suffered more from this than Britain. In little more than a generation British world power has been eclipsed and replaced by that of her ally. And though during the war the two great English-speaking nations were genuinely equal allies, even if the United States ended as by far the stronger and more dominant member of the partnership, it was only in the ensuing years of peace that Britain found herself retiring from position after position to be replaced by an American presence until she had become no more than a junior partner in the alliance.

Inside the Commonwealth American economic, political and military influence has steadily usurped British roles. Historically, arising out of the War of Independence, the United States always adopted an anti-imperial attitude whose main target was the British Empire. Suspicion of British imperialist motives at the end of the war soured relations between Roosevelt and Churchill; American pressure was constantly applied to Britain over the question of independence for India. Part of this was the result of genuine idealism; part was due to a deep-seated though usually unrecognized American jealousy of the Empire. Since 1945 the decline of British power and Britain's lessening ability either to defend its Commonwealth partners or assist them economically had led to an increasing American involvement in the affairs of the Commonwealth—at any rate in the fortunes of individual Commonwealth countries.

Thus Australia and New Zealand concluded the ANZUS Pact with the United States and thereby recognized that their safety depended upon American rather than British military might. Canada long ago accepted this and to a great extent has integrated her defence forces, in NORAD, with those of the United States and under its supreme command. Pakistan has received large shipments of American arms in its role as a SEATO power. And when in 1962 China invaded India the quantity and value of American assistance to India was far greater than Britain's.

Economically the story is the same, though, if anything, more pronounced. We have already seen the growing extent of American trade with the Commonwealth while its investment in Commonwealth countries has increased rapidly over the years. In Canada American investment is five or six times as large as Britain's (though this is exceptional and dates back a long way), while in at least one other Commonwealth country, Australia, the level of American investment (though not the total invested) now equals that of Britain. Elsewhere it is increasing in both volume and proportion. Finally, in terms of aid, the developing Commonwealth receives more from the United States than Britain, Canada, Australia and New Zealand combined can produce. The Indian and Pakistani plans would collapse without American assistance; they would survive, only dented, if Britain's aid were withdrawn; while American surplus wheat has poured into India during recent famines.

None of this growing American participation in the affairs of Commonwealth countries is necessarily unwelcome; nor could it have taken place without the consent of the countries concerned. But it does represent the omnipresent power of the United States and the consequent, inevitable attraction this has for at least certain Commonwealth countries. In Britain such American influence is often resented: partly because it signals the decline of British power and partly because the suspicion exists that the United States is consciously trying to replace British influence with her own.

The unhappy story of British Guiana between 1953 and its achievement of independence, often postponed, in 1966 and the sometimes unfair and nearly always stupid British treatment of Dr. Jagan are due in great measure to American pressures upon London because of their fears that British Guiana under Jagan would provide a Communist foothold in Latin America.

The possibility of American power and influence acting as a counterweight to Britain and the Commonwealth and seriously weakening the association in consequence is most pronounced in Canada and Australia; it is increasing in the West Indies; while elsewhere, although American policies are resented by the non-aligned members of the Commonwealth, the need for American aid is acute and could be a deciding factor in times of crisis. It is worth examining American relations with Canada and Australia in particular; and, conversely, independent Africa's determination, despite aid, to repel American political advances.

Historically, during bellicose, expansionist and anti-British moments Americans have suggested annexing Canada. But always they have regarded the land to their north as 'safe' for American investment: a natural English-speaking area for business exploitation. The investment and exploitation has certainly taken place. Holdings in Canada represent about a third of all American foreign investments and there are few Canadian industrial or financial concerns entirely free of American involvement. Oil, uranium, copper, asbestos, nickel are all 70% or more American controlled; so are many manufacturing industries. Canadian shareholders often receive their dividends in American dollars; Canadian labour organizations and unions, as branches of American ones, are run ultimately from the United States. About 70% of the Canadian economy, whether capital sources, control of business, imports or exports, is dependent upon the United States. In the circumstances it is not surprising that Canadians sometimes fear American economic takeover. This American penetration of the economy and Canadian dependence upon American participation to keep it booming are the subject of endless debates and soul-searching. Periodically, revelations of American economic control in one form or another have sparked off anti-American reactions in Canada: the late 1950's when a number of writers first revealed the extent of this dependence produced demands for a limitation upon American investment; and one of Diefenbaker's election platforms in 1958 was a 15% switch of trade to Britain and the Commonwealth. In the event little came of it. There were a few adjustments, but economic facts had to be faced and the Canadian economy remains dominated by that of the United States. So great does American preponderance sometimes appear that there are Canadians who argue that the country might as well join with the United States and make legal what is already a fact of life.

Canadian defence in Cold War terms has long been integrated with that of the United States: the various early warning systems and the 1954 North American Defense Agreement have committed Canada more or less irretrievably to ultimate sanction of American Cold War policies, however much she may protest or criticize in the meantime. In any case, as an automatic 'fly-over' target in an American/Russian nuclear war she had no choice.

Thus on Canada's side geographic proximity to the United States and the need for capital investment on a scale that no one else could provide ensured an ever closer dependence: while, for the United States, the 'safe' nature of investment in Canada, her wealth in raw materials needed by the American economy and the strategic necessity in Cold War terms of guarding Canada's 'Northern Approaches' have combined to ensure an ever more insistent American penetration of Canadian affairs. Even if Canada wanted to opt for a policy of non-alignment it is most unlikely that the United States would permit her to do so. And if Canada did have to face a choice between Commonwealth and American policies facts of dependence as well as the acceptance which has grown with proximity would almost certainly mean she would put relations with the United States first. For her, the greatest value in the British and Commonwealth relationship is that it gives some counterweight to American pressures that would otherwise prove intolerable.

Like Canada, Australia offers similar attractions to American investment. A vast and wealthy country with a small population looking for outside capital to develop its resources, its private enterprise system does not inhibit American participation, while lessening British ability to supply adequate funds left a natural opening for an American entry upon the Australian scene: this was taken after the war. Now, Australia is equally dependent upon Britain and the United States for both investment and trade: before long it is likely that the United States will have outstripped Britain. The process has been assisted by the pattern of Australian life: increasingly, as happened in Canada a long time ago, the bigness and wealth of Australia make it a natural market for American goods: an obvious example would be the greater suitability to Australian conditions of the American rather than the British car.

In the matter of defence Australia admitted as early as 1951 (ANZUS) that its future safety depended upon the United States rather than upon Britain or the Commonwealth. As a Commonwealth country which is very much aligned in the Cold War—perhaps the most belligerently anti-Communist and, of the old Dominions, the least ready to come to terms with concepts of a multiracial Commonwealth—Australia makes a natural military partner for the United States in the Pacific while her own fears of Chinese, Japanese and Indonesian numbers to her north reinforce her desire to have an alliance with a partner who will take a 'strong' line over Communist or Afro/Asian neutralist and anti-Western stances: this the United States does.

Thus, of Commonwealth countries Canada and Australia have for both defence and economic reasons been increasingly drawn within the orbit of the United States at the expense of their British and Commonwealth ties. The story may differ in other parts of the Commonwealth; not the realities of American power. Ever since the wartime destroyers for bases deal the West Indies have been uneasily aware of the fact that the United States regards them as within its sphere of influence.

In India, however, despite the size of the American aid programme, the Indian desire to remain non-aligned more than counterbalances economic dependence upon the United States. In Commonwealth Africa Britain still remains the greatest source of aid and the first trading partner, and though American aid, particularly in West Africa, has increased rapidly in recent years and the numbers of American technical assistance personnel and Peace Corps have become a major factor of influence, the African countries having just thrown off British imperialism do not intend American influence to replace it.

Now in bloc terms it may be perfectly true that neither the

Common Market nor the United States have any anti-Common-wealth policies as such. But that is not the point. What matters in the case of the Common Market is that its policies are not concerned with the Commonwealth; they are concerned with Britain and few European statesmen would be bothered by the break-up of the Commonwealth if Britain entered Europe. Consequently, should the Common Market eventually prove attractive enough for Britain to abandon other policies and join, it will have become the instrument upon which the Commonwealth could break.

The United States is the richest and most powerful nation in the world. It pursues policies conceived in its own interests—these naturally include drawing within its sphere of influence other nations or areas—Canada, Australia, the West Indies—and if in the process of doing this it weakens the Commonwealth that may be unfortunate for the weaker organization although it does not mean a conscious American design to do this.

Nonetheless, the policies of both the Common Market and the United States may well work against the interests of the Commonwealth and provide counter-attractions for its various members that prove too strong for them to resist.

REGIONAL BLOCS

Two kinds of regional groups could affect the Commonwealth: those consisting only of Commonwealth members; and those which include both Commonwealth and non-Commonwealth countries. The former kind would be unlikely to damage the Commonwealth; indeed they would strengthen it. The latter need not have adverse effects upon the association though, over the years, might detach an individual country from it.

We have already looked at the fate of Commonwealth federations and in at least two cases—Central Africa and the West Indies—economic advantage was clearly relegated to the background by political considerations. In the Asian Commonwealth the fate of Malaysia is still in the balance while the chances for some wider confederation for economic and political co-operation between

Malaysia, Indonesia and the Philippines still remains a rather vague possibility until the situation within Indonesia as well as its external intentions have become more obvious. Besides, the suggestion of Maphilindo, like Churchill's to unite Britain and France in 1940, was mooted at the height of the confrontation crisis: it is one thing to propose grandiose solutions during periods of tension; it is altogether a different matter to put them into effect when times are quieter and the peace of those concerned is no longer threatened.

The most likely possibilities of regional groupings affecting the Commonwealth are in Africa. Ideas of Pan-Africanism exercise enormous emotional appeal for the new African states. Their weakness coupled with their determination to rid themselves of the last vestiges of imperialism and the idea of African 'oneness', however unrealizable or untrue in fact, do in theory make any moves towards Pan-African co-operation attractive. And certainly, although African Commonwealth leaders have shown deep appreciation and understanding of the Commonwealth concept and its multiracial possibilities, these would still take second place should any move towards African unity become a question of practical politics. As yet there is little sign of this: African states condemn South Africa but continue their trade with her; they pass resolutions about the Congo or Rhodesia, yet between them they are unable to produce concerted action that would seriously affect the course of events.

Nonetheless, growing Pan-African sentiments coupled with economic needs and the search to expand trade and markets have led to suggestions for an East African common market. Possible members from the Commonwealth are Kenya, Uganda, Tanzania, Zambia and Malawi; from outside, Ethiopia, Somalia, Ruanda and Burundi; and it could later be expanded. Whether or not this comes into being lies in the future. Should it do so membership for a country such as Kenya need not be incompatible with membership of the Commonwealth nor work against Commonwealth interests.

However, two things have to be borne in mind. First, any form of common market requires more than simply an extensive market (as East Africa could provide); it needs also a high rate of production and considerable purchasing power. Now although certain raw

H

materials and commodities—copper in Zambia, sisal in Tanzania, coffee in Kenya—are produced in quantity they are almost entirely for export. What these countries do not yet produce themselves is a wide range of ordinary consumer goods: it is still far cheaper to import these from Britain or South Africa. Until general prosperity in the area has been considerably improved this pattern is unlikely to change greatly. Second, the political will to surrender at least certain powers to the group must also exist.

At present there is almost no evidence that any African country in fact—no matter what lip-service it pays to Pan-African theories—is prepared to surrender any of the newly acquired freedoms that have come with recent independence to a supra-national authority. Both now and into the foreseeable future African nationalism is likely to prove too strong for such measures to have any chance of success. In this respect the recent history of Commonwealth East African territories is a most useful guide. Kenya, Uganda and Tanzania had developed a whole series of common services including a single currency and customs union. Federation between them had long been regarded as practical and desirable: from time to time the British colonial authorities encouraged the idea. However, it was agreed that no formal action should be taken until all three countries were independent. Unlike Britain's Central African possessions, the three had no insuperable problems; by the time Kenya achieved independence in December 1963 the white settler minority had reconciled itself to black majority rule.

Thus, their approximate equality of size and population, the fact that they all received independence within two years of each other, and the already existing links as well as the obvious advantages that closer union would bring them should all have contributed to the formation of an East African Federation or, at the very least, closer economic co-operation. Yet if anything the contrary has been the case. Jealousy of the greater economic strength of Kenya, rivalry among the leaders and politicians, the strength of newly found nationalisms and unwillingness to surrender any powers to a central organization have not only prevented a closer union; they have led to a breakdown in some of the existing services—the end of the common currency and the growth of more individual economic policies.

Now if, after independence, nationalism is going to force apart three countries whose similarities, history and interests should all conspire to draw them closer together, and if immediate advantage will even lead them to break some of the working economic arrangements they have inherited from imperial days, there would appear to be little chance of any wider African grouping coming into being successfully, at least in the near future. Pan-Africanism may be fine in theory; nationalism comes first in practice. In all probability the same kind of nationalist considerations will prevent a similar confederation in the Malay Archipelago.

International groups of any kind are difficult enough to create or maintain. To have any chance of success they require at the very least two conditions: first, sufficient common ground—political, historical, cultural; second, powerful economic advantages. In the African case neither political similarities nor economic interest are strong enough at present to overcome nationalist individualism. It will be a long time even at the regional level, let alone on a continental scale, before Pan-Africanism can overcome the emotional desire of new African states to stand on their own and enjoy the exercise of all the freedoms independence has so recently made possible.

Just because the Commonwealth makes no centralizing demands that require surrenders of political power it is unlikely to lose its African members to new African regional groups.

Threats to the Commonwealth are more likely to come from the Common Market or the United States, whose economic power is great enough to draw into their orbits in particular Britain, Canada, Australia and the West Indies.

CHAPTER 5

Aid

EARLY expectations that a massive injection of aid from the rich nations would solve the problems of the developing countries were based upon the success of the Marshall Plan in Europe. But the analogy was false. In the case of the European countries the technology and industrialization already existed; what they needed was a single large-scale dose of assistance that would enable them to return to normal. This the United States' Marshall Aid supplied. Thereafter they managed on their own: they always possessed the necessary superstructure—government, civil service, communications, trained people.

But the problems of the developing countries were different in kind: a whole series of political and social revolutions led automatically to demands for economic progress; but in many cases there was little to build upon—no industrial base (although perhaps one or two raw materials had been mined or otherwise exploited); an inadequate system of education and few trained people with the skills appropriate to guiding modern economies; great poverty to contend with; and, above all, ways of life that would have to be drastically altered as a prerequisite of economic change.

In these circumstances aid might act as a priming factor in bringing about change but the real impetus had to be an internal one. Countries often received independence with 100 or less people holding degrees; with skeleton, half-trained civil services; and economies 80% or more based upon peasant agriculture; yet still the people expected their new governments to achieve economic and industrial revolutions in half a generation. There have been many failures and disappointments. The wonder is that so much progress has been made. In the early days of aid giving donor nations looked for quick, spectacular improvements to come from their assistance. Although in a few cases they have been agreeably surprised, more usually early enthusiasm has given place to doubts, cynicism and growing disillusionment: instead of progress one hears increasingly of corruption, inefficiency, pouring money into the 'bottomless sink of India', matching aid with achievements, exercising tighter controls to avoid waste. The high hopes with which the 'Decade of Development' started in 1960 have been replaced halfway through by growing disinterest among rich nations in giving aid at all: few have reached the target of 1% of the GNP in aid; and little effort and less imagination are being applied to the problems of the developing world. Perhaps this should cause no surprise. A rapid and successful crusade to help poor countries to develop could have sustained political interest. But the realization that the process must continue for many years, that it will be both difficult and expensive, meeting often with failure, has dampened the ardour which characterized aid-giving programmes when they started.

Instead, caution has replaced enthusiasm, 'realism' generosity, while, increasingly, donor programmes appear to be controlled by considerations of the minimum amount of assistance they can get by with giving rather than how much they should give to bring about effective development. Accepting that no quick changes can be expected, that aid is likely to remain a feature of international politics for a long time no doubt represents a realistic appraisal of facts; unfortunately it has also meant a general loss of interest and imagination among donors who now regard aid as no more than a specific aspect of their wider international programmes.

REASONS FOR AID

The motives behind aid giving are many and complex, but generally speaking can be classified under two broad headings: humanitarian and political. Whatever the value of aid programmes they have at least focused attention upon the sheer size of problems in the developing world—poverty, disease, lack of education and opportunities—and the possibility, perhaps realized for the first time, that these conditions are not necessary. Furthermore, however inadequate present aid measures may be, donor countries have also come to understand that it is within their power to alter fundamentally the conditions now existing in the developing world; that the wealth and technology possessed by a very few countries is sufficient, if correctly used, to raise substantially the living standards that prevail in the greater part of the world.

This knowledge represents the starting point for the humanitarian approach to aid; it is the argument of conscience. The rich countries have the wealth, resources and skills: they should share them with the poor. Now communications have so shrunk the world that no part can any longer be isolated from the rest, there is a greater urgency to find a single world approach. The inequalities and dangers of a world divided into 'rich' and 'poor' are further emphasized by the startling differences between the two extremes: the wealth of the United States and Canada is so great, and the wretched poverty in India so crippling to either progress or human values that it has become increasingly difficult for a wealthy nation to disclaim any responsibility.

So in humanitarian terms it is argued that a moral responsibility lies upon the rich few to assist the poor majority, if not to become rich, at least to achieve economic break-throughs that will make possible tolerable living standards. No doubt international politics of the mid-twentieth century have assisted the growth of a humanitarian desire to help the poor countries overcome their problems. The Cold War, constant tensions, the threat of nuclear destruction have made people feel increasingly remote from the business of government: there is little they can do. Helplessness in face of these issues has added point to a field of activity in which the individual can still be involved. And so the humanitarian motive to help, because aid is needed and can be given, has become a genuine factor of importance influencing relations between rich and poor nations. In consequence, idealism and conscience have combined. Modern media of communications have made the problems clear enough, and the younger generation in particular, often cynically disinterested in politics, is prepared to devote time and energy to assisting those less fortunate than themselves—hence the popularity of the various Western volunteer movements.

Little about the humanitarian motive is straightforward: 'do-gooding'; an uneasy conscience about past imperial exploitation; a sense of guilt at having too much wealth when so many have virtually nothing; the desire for a better world; and mixed with all these slightly vague reasons are others less admirable—complexes concerned with passing on the benefits of 'superior' cultures, an attitude that still, unfortunately, characterizes too much of the West's aid giving. It is easy to sneer at humanitarian motives but they do represent an important aspect of aid giving and one that politicians are quick enough to use when it suits them to do so. However, such good intentions alone would have made little impact. Aid exists on the scale it does for political reasons.

The Cold War really ushered in the 'aid age' and during the early years of tensions between East and West when both sides hoped to win to their cause the non-aligned they began to use aid as a major instrument of policy. But the early expectations that a country could be bought if enough assistance was offered were soon destroyed by the firm insistence upon 'no strings' that uncommitted nations, led by India, maintained. Nonetheless aid has still been used as a weapon of diplomacy ever since. Its application can be classified under three heads: politics, self-interest and world stability, although these divisions overlap and may appear to be artificial.

Political or diplomatic aid is that given in the old sense: helping friends, gaining new ones, keeping doubtful allies in line, buying services or—negatively—withdrawing support as a punishment: in other words, aid as an instrument of policy used to manoeuvre weaker countries according to the international objectives of the donor. It has had remarkably little impact in this sense: no country has changed sides or abandoned non-alignment because of aid received, although remarkable results have been obtained by non-aligned countries playing upon these motives of the donors.

Self-interest represents the more exact economic sense of obtaining advantage in a particular country: trade as the result of tied aid, markets following the supply of particular goods or equipment, investment opportunities—in other words, the skilful provision of aid can make an economy dependent upon the donor. In British/ Commonwealth terms, for example, India and Nigeria both represent huge potential future markets and it can be plausibly argued that large scale British aid to them in the 1960's will help establish markets oriented towards British goods for the 1970's and 1980's.

World stability: it makes sound sense to give aid so as to even out extremes of poverty; otherwise the desperation of the very poor may either spark off revolutionary tendencies dangerous to the *status quo* desired by the richer countries; alternatively, such countries left unaided by the West may become the special objects of Communist assistance and so, once again, we come full circle to Cold War reasoning.

These are only the more obvious motives of a long list. Prestige or keeping up with the international Joneses is also an important reason for aid: if the United States seriously increases its effort almost certainly Britain, West Germany and the others will follow suit—so will the Russians—since the amount of aid given has now become a measure of great power status.

Politicians always play down these political motives and insist upon high principles: moral responsibility and the desire to assist developing countries make genuine economic progress. In part this is true since stability may well follow the resolution of economic and other problems in the developing world and this is—apparently—in the interests of the donor countries. Yet all too often the political aims of the donors rather than the economic needs of the recipients guide the kind and amount of aid that is given.

In terms of Commonwealth aid it is worth examining a few examples. We have already seen how the Colombo Plan came into being (see above, pages 35–38); this represents an approach to aid least tainted by motives of political or economic self-interest among the donors. Rarely, however, has this standard been maintained. Britain has adopted a policy of making a parting gift to each of her colonies when they have achieved independence: this has consisted in part of any balances already voted under C.D. & W. funds, in part of a new loan, sometimes of an outright grant. Now a comparison of the treatment she gave Kenya and Tanganyika is interesting. In the case of Kenya the long Mau Mau crisis and the presence of a significant white settler minority with powerful advocates lobbying for them in Whitehall meant a very generous aid settlement and subsequent large sums of money for the Kenya Government to use in compensating white farmers whose land was to be bought out. In other words, a colony that had been a trouble spot could expect (and got) generous British aid. For her own political reasons Britain did not want further difficulties or recriminations after independence had been granted.

On the other hand, Tanganyika had given no trouble in the years before independence; the consequence was that Britain—using the current economic crisis as an excuse—made a miserable parting offer of only half the amount that had been promised originally. Only after Nyerere had spoken of British meanness and the Governor, Sir Richard Turnbull, had flown to London to lobby ministers in a last bid to avert a crisis was the Government finally persuaded to change its mind: then, a more reasonable settlement followed. This comparison illustrates a simple principle as far as Britain and her one-time colonies have been concerned: the more trouble a would-be recipient threatens to cause the greater its expectations of aid are likely to be. Thus, Britain paid to save herself the embarrassment of appearing mean in the case of Tanganyika and gave generously in the case of Kenya because of the more powerful pressures that could be applied to her.

The political nature of aid can be clearly seen in Britain's treatment of the proposed 'Tanzam' railway scheme. For eighteen months Zambia kept pressing for assistance to build a rail link from Lusaka to Dar-es-Salaam; Britain put forward every political and economic argument why the project was unnecessary, unfeasible and a waste of money. Then, during the Commonwealth Prime Ministers' Conference of 1965 Chou en-Lai offered Chinese assistance to build the entire railway (whether China in fact could do so is another matter). The point is that within a week Britain and Canada agreed to finance a survey while all the arguments that Britain had advanced over the previous eighteen months apparently became invalid the moment the Chinese offer was made.

When Indonesian confrontation appeared to have come to an end Britain offered a loan of £1 million to Indonesia at a time when she was arguing her inability to give more aid to Malaysia. All these examples demonstrate only too clearly the political nature of aid giving; there is little wonder if poor countries have become cynical about the intentions of donors.

As always, the motives behind aid are mixed; but the prime consideration is political advantage—the self-interest of the donor. And this of course is as true of Commonwealth countries—Britain, Canada, Australia and New Zealand—as of any others. They aid the developing countries because they believe it is in their interest to do so. Subsequently they rationalize their action in terms of altruism. It is natural that the bulk of British aid goes to the developing countries of the Commonwealth since her interest in their fortunes is far greater than in most other parts of the developing world; to a lesser extent this is true of Canada, Australia and New Zealand. All have the added advantage of working in countries where Commonwealth links and the habit of co-operation make the aid-giving process technically easier to do anyway. But this does not alter the basic motives of self-interest that lie behind the giving.

The recipients of aid include a high proportion of new countries which, for this reason, may be less practised in the diplomatic arts of pushing their own interests than are aid donors, although they learn fast enough. Their motives for receiving aid may be fewer than those for giving it; but the variety of sources from which they manage to extract assistance demonstrate a rapid and successful appreciation of their own bargaining powers. No developing country wants aid in the sense of liking the dependence upon the donor implied in receiving his assistance. They take aid to survive; because the rapid economic progress that their people demand can only be achieved with such outside help; because they often feel that such aid is 'owed' to them (the case of ex-colonies and their past imperial masters); and because they have learnt their own bargaining strength. Realizing the motives that persuade donor countries to give aid, the recipients have no qualms in playing upon such political reasons of self-interest in order to obtain all the help they can from whatever source. In the circumstances they feel fully justified (and no doubt are) in demanding a minimum of strings, in using 'blackmail' tactics, in playing one side in the Cold War off against the other and so on. Despite all this it is worth bearing in mind that no country wants to be dependent upon the bounty of another since, as long as this is the case, it can hardly claim genuine independence—and this is the first desire of all nations.

Now as an introduction to Commonwealth co-operation in the field of aid this may appear an unnecessarily long discussion of the reasons for aid giving and receiving in general. The point is that in the Commonwealth as in the world at large the basic motives in operation are the same and self-interest comes first. Britain, Canada, Australia and New Zealand give most of their aid to the Commonwealth primarily because they believe it to be to their advantage to do so. Commonwealth ties help the process: they make it easier and more attractive; they provide ready (and suitably moral) justifications—building the multiracial association and putting the group first; and the inter-Commonwealth aid effort can be presented as one more valuable Commonwealth link. Yet much of it would go on anyway since the same reasons for aid would operate whether or not the Commonwealth existed: it so happens that the Commonwealth includes among its members a large proportion of the poor developing countries in the world.

Thus it would be unrealistic to say that the Commonwealth itself is responsible for the aid that passes between its members. What the Commonwealth does do is provide a focus and natural area for aid from its rich members while the already operating habits of working together make inter-Commonwealth aid a relatively easy field of further co-operation. The fact that aid activities present one of the happier areas of Commonwealth co-operation should not be interpreted to mean more than it does. Aid certainly provides a powerful Commonwealth link and should not be neglected as such; but sentiment apart, the main reasons for aid from one Commonwealth country to another are simply their advantage as they see it.

KINDS OF AID

Aid is given in a variety of ways; all the methods outlined below are used by Britain and the other three rich Commonwealth countries.

1. *The grant:* an outright gift of money, normally given for a specific purpose, sometimes as general budgetary support. It represents the most generous form of financial assistance since it neither has to be paid back nor involves the recipient in payments of interest. The drawback for the recipient, however, is that the donor of a grant often feels a greater right to dictate how it should be used.

2. *Loans:* these may be classified as interest free—Britain started making such loans in 1965: 'soft' loans with interest set at low rates of 2–3%; and 'hard' loans that carry the going rate of interest, sometimes as high as 6–7%. Loans are often tied to the purchase of goods in the donor country and this may considerably reduce their value: if for example Britain makes a loan, part or all of which is conditional upon buying her goods, a recipient may find it could obtain a third as much equipment again if it were free to spend the money in East Germany or Czechoslovakia instead of in Britain. However, the harder a loan the greater freedom it usually confers: a recipient who has to pay back both the loan and high interest over the years feels free to use the money as it wishes. The drawback to recipients of loans lies in the interest repayments: a country such as India, which has received vast loans over the years, now faces a situation in which a great proportion of its foreign earnings are eaten away simply paying interest (and capital repayments) on past loans, while the tragic-comic situation has almost been reached in which she must ask for further loans simply to pay interest on those that already exist. Nor must it be forgotten that aid donors are now receiving back from recipients substantial annual sums in repayment.

3. *Technical assistance:* in many respects this is the most important form of aid. Although they lack capital most developing countries are even shorter of skills and the trained people who can make their

economic plans work—sometimes it is simply a question of keeping
government machinery functioning efficiently—as well as training
their own nationals to do the jobs in the future. Technical assistance
concerns the loaning of people: the provision of 'experts' at various
levels from the schoolteacher to the director of economic planning.
Technical assistance personnel either fill gaps and perform specific
jobs necessary for the recipient's economic progress, or they train
the local people. More usually they combine the two activities.

4. *Training* : although this is really an aspect of technical assistance
one part of it can be separated from the rest and that is the provision
of training in the donor country: the granting of scholarships or
bursaries to train in Britain or Canada, for example. There are large
numbers of 'students' ranging from undergraduates at universities or
technical colleges and technicians in industry to older and often
highly qualified government administrators on special courses of
instruction not available in their own countries. The value of bringing people for training from a developing country to a highly advanced
donor nation can be considerable, often providing many benefits of
cultural or maturing experience apart from the course itself; sometimes, however, the effects can be damaging, especially for younger
students, since in a rich country they come to accept and expect
standards that do not exist at home and on their return they become
dissatisfied with the conditions in which they must work.

5. *Volunteers:* although they should be classified as technical
assistance they deserve a category on their own, both because of the
motives persuading them to give service in developing countries and
because their cost is often—though not always—lower than that of
normal technical assistance personnel. The advantage of volunteers
lies in their freedom from the more narrow attitudes associated with
professional technical assistance men; their willingness to turn their
hands to a wide variety of activities; and their genuine success in
being accepted on a basis of easy equality by the people with whom
they work in the developing countries. The disadvantage to recipients

generally lies in their lower level of technical skills, lack of experience and the short time for which they stay.

6. *Trade concessions:* the long-term aim of all aid programmes ought to be creating the economic conditions that will make it possible for the developing countries to stand on their own as normal trading partners with the rest of the world. Certainly, all are probably genuine when they say they would prefer trade to aid. Unfortunately, most developing countries' trade depends upon raw materials and commodities such as sugar or cocoa—all notoriously subject to price fluctuations—or upon the manufacture of relatively simple goods such as textiles. Aid in building up a new industry is of small value if subsequently markets for its products are not available when it attempts to export them. In this respect British quota allowances for Commonwealth textiles—particularly from India, Pakistan and Hong Kong—have proved one of the most valuable forms of aid she has given. The Commonwealth Sugar Agreement whereby Britain has guaranteed to buy fixed quantities of sugar at above world prices has been another. The difficulties involved in this form of aid are most concerned with pressures from business interests within the donor countries themselves.

There are other types of aid, including military assistance, but those listed above are the main ones. Commonwealth aid is given in a number of ways: bilaterally—that is, by direct arrangements worked out between donor and recipient; multilaterally—through organizations such as the Colombo Plan or through consortia such as that for India in which Commonwealth countries are a minority in numbers and even more in terms of the value of their contributions as compared with the total; while all Commonwealth countries contribute to the various world organizations: the World Bank, the United Nations Special Fund, the International Development Association and the other specialized agencies.

THE GENERAL FLOW OF AID

Out of the total flow of aid from rich to poor countries (excluding the Communist bloc) the Commonwealth share in 1963 was only

9·5%; while in terms of aid received by developing countries members of the Commonwealth received 30% of their bilateral assistance from their Commonwealth partners (Britain, Canada, Australia and New Zealand) while the balance came from non-Commonwealth sources. Although since 1963 all four rich Commonwealth countries have substantially increased the flow of their aid and are now probably contributing a figure nearer 12% of total non-Communist aid, the above figures illustrate two main points.

First, Commonwealth needs are far greater than Commonwealth aid resources and more than two-thirds of them have to be found from outside the association. Second, the rich Commonwealth nations are not the most generous aid donors on a *per capita* basis. Though between them the four could never come near meeting the total needs of their developing partners, they could provide far more than they do at present.

By far the largest aid donor in the world is the United States and this includes aid to the Commonwealth, particularly India and Pakistan. Of other major donors France still devotes nearly all her resources to her own ex-colonies; West Germany is now a substantial source of aid to Commonwealth countries and especially to India; Japan's contribution to Asian countries is growing rapidly; while, of Communist countries, Russia's stake in the Indian sub-continent is now of great importance.

In general terms American aid is to be found virtually everywhere; not surprisingly, though, India and Pakistan are the biggest Commonwealth recipients of her assistance. Communist aid is given on a highly selective political basis—India, Pakistan and Ceylon are again major recipients of it, Africa increasingly though still on a small scale; Chinese aid in East Africa is in fact very small in quantity though the publicity attached to it has become disproportionate.

So vast are India's problems that the aid she receives from all sources is barely adequate to keep her development plans operational; all four Commonwealth donor countries give substantial proportions of their aid to her yet it represents only a small part of the total India receives. In the long run the success or failure of India's development, dependent as it is upon so much outside assistance, may well prove to be the touchstone upon which aid programmes in general are adjudged to have succeeded or not. So far the Commonwealth and particularly Britain has done nothing like enough to help the largest and poorest of all the developing countries (apart from China); and if there is to be any successful Commonwealth aid programme far greater attention and effort must be concentrated upon India than is at present the case.

The general pattern of Commonwealth aid giving is well defined. The four donor countries are all involved in assistance programmes to the Asian members—India, Pakistan, Ceylon and Malaysia—and this involvement reflects both the size of the problems on the Indian sub-continent and the strategic importance attached to these countries by the Commonwealth as a whole and especially by Australia and New Zealand. Britain is the only one of the four whose aid goes to all Commonwealth countries, and for the African Commonwealth, especially East and Central Africa, she is still by far the largest single source of assistance; this is also true for the Caribbean Commonwealth. Apart from her Asian commitments Canada concentrates her Commonwealth aid in West Africa—Nigeria and Ghana—and the Caribbean, while Australia and New Zealand give the balance of theirs to their various dependencies: New Guinea and Papua and the islands of Oceania. The greatest part of all the aid from the four goes into the Commonwealth.

About 10% of British aid and roughly comparable shares of the other three countries' totals are given in contributions to the various United Nations' special agencies or through other multilateral programmes; a considerable amount of this will eventually find its way into Commonwealth countries. In this area at least most of the developing Commonwealth countries are also donors as well as recipients: they support the various United Nations' aid agencies, sometimes with substantial and not just token contributions, while in one or two cases and notably India they supply a fair number of personnel as technical assistance experts for the different world programmes.

It is worth noting here one of the great discussion points about aid. Most developing countries would prefer to see all aid administered through the United Nations. This is understandable enough: the world body, they feel, would be impartial; to a large extent aid could then be removed from politics; the bilateral bargaining and 'blackmails' would disappear; and above all recipients would find it far easier and less galling to their pride to receive assistance from the United Nations instead of constantly being reminded of their dependence upon individual donors. Aid through the United Nations could not be used as a political weapon by donors seeking advantage and influence for themselves. In idealistic terms this is undoubtedly the best answer. Unfortunately the weakness of such an approach is its failure to take into account the very reasons why aid is given at all. Donor countries which are quite prepared to give assistance when they can receive the political and moral credit for doing so as well as reaping economic and other advantages would become far more reluctant if their contributions all went into a United Nations pool and they could not claim that any particular programme existed because of their efforts. However justifiable in theory, in practice, should this recipient desire for all aid to be channelled through the United Nations ever be accepted the inevitable result would be a diminution of the total given. Moreover, poor countries would lose one of their most potent bargaining weapons. It is one thing for a Commonwealth country to approach Britain and argue, for example: West Germany is giving us more aid than you and we were once your colony; or the Communists are gaining markets because their assistance is greater than yours—such tactics may shame or spur Britain into greater effort. It is quite a different matter for the developing countries to appeal in general terms, as they would have to, for more generous donor contributions to a United Nations fund: such appeals rarely have much force. Since self-interest represents the most powerful motive for aid giving it is wise for would-be recipients to maintain the bilateral relationship.

COMMONWEALTH NEEDS

United Nations statistics for 1963 showed that the Commonwealth then accounted for 785 million people out of a world total of 3160

J

million—almost exactly a quarter of the world's population. But of the 785 million only 86 million, the populations of Britain, Canada, Australia and New Zealand, could be considered as developed while 699 million were recipients of aid. They represented 32% or just under a third of the world's developing population. The four rich Commonwealth countries only represent 8·6% of the developed world—the potential aid givers. These figures clearly demonstrate how the development problems of the Commonwealth are too great to be tackled by the Commonwealth alone. It is hardly to be expected that 8·6% of the developed, potential donor countries can shoulder 32% of the world's aid needs. This is not to say that rich Commonwealth countries are doing all they could or should to help the developing world; but it does mean that Commonwealth needs far outstrip the Commonwealth ability to meet them.

The aid needs of Commonwealth countries are vast. India alone, with a population that has just passed the 500 million mark and a *per capita* income of only £26 a year, presents the greatest single development problem in the world (outside China) and can absorb far more aid than at present it receives. But at least India did start independence with a great advantage: it had a sound superstructure of government, communications and adequate numbers of trained people in both the civil service and the professions. Its greatest need has always been for capital; its most urgent problems where technical assistance can be most valuable lie in the two fields of modernizing agriculture and birth control. Second only to India in the Commonwealth (and also in world terms excepting possibly Indonesia) comes Pakistan with a population of approximately 100 million and a *per capita* income of about £28 a year. As one of the successor states to British India it also inherited a proportion of the British superstructure of government, though it did less well out of the partition than India. Its problems are on a comparable scale, its *per capita* income about the same and its aid requirements similar to those of India.

On the whole the Asian Empire inherited from Britain at least reasonable government machineries in terms of the numbers of trained civil servants and other skilled personnel; India already had a considerable industrial base; Malaya had the twin commodities, highly developed, of tin and rubber; Singapore had long been one of the world's great entrepôts; while Pakistan and Ceylon, if less well endowed, did have reasonable raw materials and plantation industries.

The development of the African Commonwealth had followed different lines. Only in colonies of white settlement—Kenya, Rhodesia and Zambia—had any substantial industry developed before independence: of these, the emphasis of white settler effort in Kenya had been on agriculture; Zambia's copper provided one of the largest industries on the whole continent but otherwise the country had almost no industrial development. Nigeria has recently discovered oil, but generally speaking the African pattern is based upon agriculture, often single-crop economies: cocoa and palm oils in West Africa, sisal, coffee and cotton in East Africa, copper and tobacco in Central Africa, cattle in Bechuanaland.*

There is considerable variation of wealth as between one Commonwealth African country and another, Ghana with a *per capita* income now exceeding £70 a year heading the list, Tanzania and Uganda with about the same—£28 per head—at the bottom. Most need capital assistance: Ghana for its Volta development scheme, Nigeria for its oil, though in time these will both be major sources of revenue; Zambian copper revenues make her a weaker candidate for capital than Malawi or Tanzania, though she still needs it. But the greatest aid requirement of Commonwealth Africa is for technical assistance. Unlike her achievement in India, Britain did not attempt any real policy of Africanization in the civil services of East and Central Africa until within a few years of independence; nor had education been developed sufficiently at the secondary and university level. Consequently, when independence came, these countries found themselves desperately short of trained personnel at almost every level: civil service; education; business. This need is reflected by the distribution of British technical assistance personnel overseas: of 12,527 British personnel serving in Commonwealth countries at the end of 1964, 7379 were to be found in four African territories—Kenya, Uganda, Tanzania and Zambia.

* Now Botswana.

The special problems facing the three High Commission territories —Bechuanaland, Basutoland and Swaziland—dominated as they are by their proximity to and dependence upon the South African economy, are still further enhanced by their povery and their lack of trained people. In 1965 Bechuanaland's sole source of revenue, its cattle, was virtually annihilated by the drought, while it had only twenty-six sixth-formers in the whole country. Malawi appears likely to be dependent upon British bounty simply to run normal government services, apart from any development, into the foreseeable future while Gambia can hardly claim economic viability.

In the Commonwealth Caribbean, although both Jamaica and Trinidad have made valiant and successful efforts to diversify and build up a number of light industries in addition to Jamaican bauxite and Trinidad oil refining, the smaller islands, despite the Commonwealth Sugar Agreement and tourism, have almost no prospects of industrialization: they are overpopulated; poor; and dependent upon aid, mainly from Britain.

Commonwealth aid problems may be summarized as follows. First, of the twenty-three independent Commonwealth countries (summer 1966) only four—Britain, Canada, Australia and New Zealand—can be classified as donor nations; of the other nineteen all qualify in some degree as aid recipients—India as the greatest in the world, Cyprus as a marginal case at the other end. Moreover, the remaining colonial territories and dependencies also qualify for and are in receipt of aid, mainly from Britain but from Australia and New Zealand in Oceania and from Canada in the West Indies. Between them these Commonwealth recipients represent a third of the world's developing nations requiring assistance.

Second, all need capital: the requirements of some such as India and Pakistan are so large that they are barely met by world consortia, let alone from the rich Commonwealth countries; other such as Zambia can and are expected to produce most of their capital requirements out of their own revenues but could still use funds from outside; and a few, notably Malawi, cannot even meet budgetary expenses without external assistance.

Third, all again require technical assistance: but whereas the two Asian giants are relatively well off in producing their own skilled manpower, though still desperately short, here the greatest need is to be found in East and Central Africa, the former British territories where least was done to train the local people to take over from the colonial authorities when independence came; in this respect the West Indies, with a longer educational tradition, come out surprisingly well.

Fourth, special problems requiring emergency aid measures constantly arise to upset the general pattern: UDI and the need for additional assistance to enable Zambia to withstand the crisis strains upon her economy; Indonesian confrontation and the need for military and economic assistance to enable Malaysia to remain intact in the face of the threat; drought in Bechuanaland; famine in India*, etc.

Fifth, an unhappy but politically predictable aid pattern: the complaint of the small territories that they are constantly neglected and given minimum assistance in answer to all their requests, usually because they have neither the ability to cause sufficient trouble nor the economic and strategic importance or lobbying power necessary to attract more than token gestures of aid. Sierra Leone, Gambia, the West Indies and the High Commission territories have all felt themselves victims of this treatment from time to time; so have others.

However the problem is viewed Commonwealth aid needs will continue; in many cases (due to population explosion or lack of any resources) they may well increase into the foreseeable future. The aim of the developing countries is to reach the so-called point of economic take-off: that is, achieve the capacity to generate sufficient of their own capital as well as training enough of their own personnel that they no longer need rely upon assistance from outside. For most of them this day is still far distant. The aim of the donor countries—despite all the political and economic advantages they may seek in the process—should be to help the recipients of aid reach the take-off point as soon as possible so that they not only achieve their ostensible

* See footnote, page 43.

aim but also relieve themselves of the burden of supplying aid indefinitely.

The difficulties for both are immense, while discouragements may sometimes tempt donors to abandon their aid programmes altogether. What is needed above all is a change of attitude. At present the normal donor approach to aid is: how much can we afford to give? Instead, it should be: how much is needed to do the job?

THE COMMONWEALTH AID EFFORT

In 1964 total aid of all kinds—grants, loans, technical assistance—made available by the four Commonwealth donors amounted to approximately £280 million, and of this £218 million or more than 75% went to the Commonwealth. Some £21 million of their aid was in the form of multilateral grants to world agencies and a proportion of this would also have reached Commonwealth countries.

If this aid is broken down into its three divisions: bilateral loans and grants; technical assistance personnel; and training facilities, then the Commonwealth picture is as follows—of British aid, 88% of its bilateral loans and grants, 95% of its technical assistance personnel and 71% of its training awards went to Commonwealth countries; comparable figures for Canada are 64%, 81% and 74%; for Australia 91%, 62% (although this excludes the figures for its dependencies of Papua and New Guinea) and 61%; and for New Zealand 86%, 96% and 77%.

This concentration of their aid upon the Commonwealth is natural enough: first because the developing members of the Commonwealth represent in any case a large proportion of the total in need of assistance; second, because other Commonwealth links—language, common forms of government procedure and so on—make co-operation over the giving and administration of aid easier for both sides.

Nearly all this aid is on a bilateral basis—a Commonwealth donor giving direct assistance to a Commonwealth recipient—rather than by means of any joint consultative organizations acting on behalf of the Commonwealth as a whole. There are some multilateral approaches to aid and certain bodies are used for this purpose. Yet, bodies such as the Commonwealth Economic Committee, the Commonwealth Education Liaison Committee or the Agricultural Bureau function entirely in a consultative role and have no aid funds to distribute. The Colombo Plan starting as a Commonwealth venture in 1950 and subsequently embracing non-Commonwealth countries in South-East Asia as well, and the Commonwealth Scholarship and Fellowship Plan for educational exchanges between Commonwealth countries emerging from the 1959 Montreal Conference are examples of joint Commonwealth planning; yet, in both cases, the aid and scholarships given have been arranged almost entirely on a bilateral basis as between two Commonwealth countries.

They illustrate an important aspect of Commonwealth co-operation in this as in other fields: Commonwealth members generally are quite willing to meet together as a group and examine joint problems and suggest solutions; but when it comes to implementation they nearly always prefer—partly for administrative reasons, partly because there still appears to remain an underlying fear of any centralizing tendency—to work on a strictly bilateral basis. Thus in general there is a high degree of co-operation between donor and recipient countries on a bilateral basis but not a great deal on a group basis. This is both shortsighted and a waste of obvious, already existing means of collaboration.

A brief examination of aid figures relating to India can be taken to indicate the size of Commonwealth aid problems and the rich Commonwealth's ability to meet them. Up to the end of 1963 India had received a total of £2378·3 million aid from all sources: £239 million of this had been in grant form, the rest—£2139·3 million—as loans. Of this, the total from the four Commonwealth donor countries, both grants and loans, amounted to no more than £333·3 million or less than 15%. At the same time India had received £814 million or over 33% of its aid from the United States; major funds had also come from the World Bank (£302 million), Russia (£288 million), West Germany (£271 million), the International Development Association (£107 million). Thus the Commonwealth comes a very poor second to the United States and is not much greater as a source of funds than the World Bank, Russia or West Germany. Of this Commonwealth total the British share amounts to £205 million, which puts her fifth on the list of contributors, not a comparison that does her particular credit.

The direction and amounts of Commonwealth aid are as follows. First, Britain. In 1964 Britain spent £189 million in aid; the figure for 1965 was approximately £200 million and in 1966 it may reach £225 million. Excepting that 10% of her aid goes to multilateral organizations and a further 10% to foreign countries, the balance, 80%, is spent in the Commonwealth. The largest recipients of British aid in 1964 were India (£35 million) and Pakistan (£10 million), representing the sheer size of their development problems; Kenya (£15 million)—a more complicated case due partly to the importance placed upon the country in African strategic terms by Britain and partly because of the obligation assumed by Britain to finance the 'buying out' of white settler farmers; and Malawi (£11 million), reflecting the country's desperate poverty and absolute need and Britain's sense of continuing obligation to a past colony that remains economically non-viable after independence. The balance of British financial assistance was widely distributed throughout the Commonwealth.

Similarly in 1964, of more than 13,000 British technical assistance personnel, over 12,500 were in the Commonwealth and of these 7379 were in four countries—Kenya, Uganda, Tanzania and Zambia. This heavy concentration of British personnel in East and Central Africa reflects both the magnitude of their needs and the earlier failure (before independence) on the part of the British colonial authorities to do a better job in training their successors.

Finally, from a total of 3629 government-sponsored training places for students from developing countries in Britain, 71% were from Commonwealth countries. However, there are (1966) nearly 70,000 overseas students of all kinds studying in Britain, the bulk of them from developing Commonwealth countries, and the generous provision of places in British establishments of higher education (something like 10% of the total available) is a major aid contribution.

Apart from government, private sources of aid—churches and missionary societies; bodies such as Oxfam, War on Want; the volunteer organizations such as VSO and foundations—are variously estimated to produce assistance worth between £10 million and £20 million a year. Once more the bulk of this goes to the Commonwealth.

Second, Canada. In 1964 the total value of her aid was £46·6 million of which £26·5 million went to Commonwealth countries. Canada's areas of concentration in the Commonwealth are far narrower than Britain's: £21·4 million of the above sum went to India and Pakistan alone, while Nigeria, Ghana and the West Indies are the other major recipients of Canadian assistance. Canadian technical assistance personnel are also largely concentrated in the Commonwealth—of 409 under bilateral programmes in 1964, 332 were serving in Commonwealth countries, while 74% of Canadian training places offered to developing countries were held by Commonwealth students.

Third, Australia. Australian aid is directed almost exclusively to South and South-East Asia. Out of a total of £38·3 million aid during the financial year 1964/65 more than £26 million went to the Australian dependencies of Papua and New Guinea as grants; the balance went to South and South-East Asian countries—in particular India, Pakistan and Malaysia from the Commonwealth, Thailand and Vietnam of non-Commonwealth countries. Australian technical assistance follows the same pattern and of 935 training places in Australia, 635 (66%) were held by Commonwealth students.

Finally, of the rich Commonwealth countries, New Zealand aid (£4·3 million in 1964) goes first to her Pacific dependencies—Cook Islands, Niue, Western Samoa; second to Malaysia, Pakistan and India. The distribution of New Zealand technical assistance and the award of training places also follow the pattern of the other three and are mainly confined to Commonwealth countries.

The developing Commonwealth countries, particularly India, also give aid, mainly in the form of contributions to multilateral organizations—the World Bank and IDA—or by supplying technical assistance personnel, especially through the United Nations' programmes.

India increasingly in recent years has been offering training scholarships to members of the African Commonwealth.

Now a summary of the British, Canadian, Australian and New Zealand aid effort shows that of all kinds—financial, technical assistance and training, the bulk—roughly 80%—goes to their developing Commonwealth partners. But none of the four has yet achieved the modest 'Development Decade' target of 1% GNP in aid: Britain is currently giving no more than 0·67% of her GNP in total government aid; Australia about the same proportion; Canada only 0·4%; New Zealand less than 0·3%. In other words, the four rich Commonwealth donors can hardly claim to be generous in terms of their own wealth; still less in terms of the absolute needs of poor countries whether Commonwealth or not.

A COMMONWEALTH AID PLAN

A study of Commonwealth aid practices reveals several factors of importance. First, although there may be a high degree of co-operation bilaterally as between a Commonwealth donor and the recipient of its aid, there is not a great deal of group co-operation in this field, even taking such organizations as the Colombo Plan and Commonwealth Scholarship and Fellowship Scheme into account. Second, the four Commonwealth donor nations are not particularly generous as aid givers when compared with world efforts: France has a far better record than any other country, having reached a figure of 1·3% of her GNP which is devoted to aid, while Japan, still a relatively poor country, is making remarkable efforts to increase its aid programmes. Of the Commonwealth countries, on the other hand Britain constantly pleads other world commitments or balance of payment crises as reasons why she cannot improve her effort; the narrow concentration of Australian aid shows how much her political concern with her own safety in South-East Asia dominates what she does; while Canada and New Zealand with *per capita* incomes that place them almost at the top of the world in terms of wealth could certainly afford to do more. Third, however much the wealthy Commonwealth countries increase their effort and even if they

concentrated it entirely upon the Commonwealth, it is still obvious that they could not meet more than a proportion of the total aid needs of developing Commonwealth countries.

In the light of such limitations it could be argued that any attempt at a concerted Commonwealth approach to aid would be a waste of time; but to do so would be an admission, if not of defeat, certainly of complacency. The above three points are worth considering in more detail.

The lack of a concerted approach to aid problems is partly the result of past imperial practices, and partly a simple waste of joint consultative means that already exist. The achievement of independence by the old Dominions and, in the later post-war era, of the new Commonwealth was not unnaturally attended by determined efforts to resist any centralizing tendencies which were then regarded with suspicion as British attempts to maintain some form of imperial control; but it makes no sense to allow such former suspicions to inhibit possibly valuable joint co-operation in the present age, especially over something as important and needed as aid.

The lack of generosity in the aid efforts of the four can be altered quickly enough if a change of attitude towards aid can be produced. The will to accomplish the job has to be substituted for the present less admirable approach that seems to be governed by political considerations of the minimum a donor can get away with. The United Nations' target of 1% GNP is only a figure and could be replaced by quite different criteria. The point is to have a target at which to aim.

The fact that the rich four can never supply all Commonwealth needs does not mean that working as a group they could not produce more effective aid programmes than at present. Indeed, a Commonwealth multilateral approach to aid offers very great opportunities to improve aid techniques generally, to spur Commonwealth countries into greater efforts and to provide an example of co-operation that could influence the whole pattern of aid giving throughout the world.

No one disputes the need to assist developing countries; and the rich members of the Commonwealth have all accepted a responsibility to do so. Unfortunately too much of their effort is haphazard: the *ad hoc* response to a crisis instead of being part of a longer term plan. Thus Indonesian confrontation leads to a general increase of aid to Malaysia; famine in India to special emergency relief measures; a Chinese aid offer to Britain taking action where before she had denied the necessity and ability to do so. Half the time it requires a crisis before reasonable and effective action is taken and this kind of approach only emphasizes the political nature of aid giving in general: it appears rapidly and in large amounts when donor interests are involved; in small amounts if at all when this is not the case.

Early approaches to aid showed considerable imagination and enthusiasm. But the recognition that aid giving was to be a long process with no quick results tended to dampen former enthusiasm as well as the sense of urgency. No doubt this was inevitable when aid took its place as a normal aspect of international relations; but it happens also because donors are too concerned with immediate political reasons for giving aid rather than with long-term objectives. An imaginative joint Commonwealth approach to aid problems could produce major advances in the whole field of international assistance. They are much needed. But the trouble about imagination is that it usually also requires courage since innovations are involved; and courage, all too frequently, is not a prominent element in aid programmes. Too often a donor will wait to see what other donor nations are doing, fearful that, if alone of rich countries it embarks upon a new aid policy, somehow its rivals will take advantage of it rather than follow suit. Thus, Whitehall civil servants seemed more frightened that Britain's generous policy of interest free-loans announced in 1965 would mean that her money would be used to pay back interest on loans from other donor countries (the U.S.A. or West Germany) who were not following suit than whether or not it would be of assistance to recipient countries.

If the Commonwealth as a body were to recognize two main aims—the achievement of some basic minimal standard by all its members, and the fact that every country would prefer to substitute trade for aid—then, by consciously working towards these objectives the rich four could greatly increase their own contributions and effectiveness as donors while also stimulating world efforts to solve the problems of developing countries. Four aspects of Commonwealth aid are worth particular attention: areas of concentration; commodity agreements; the provision of markets for the developing members; and a joint approach to aid.

1. The first suggestion, areas of concentration, is the simplest; it exists in part already. At present only British aid is spread widely throughout the Commonwealth while that of the other three tends to be concentrated in particular areas. The greatest burden for aid in the Commonwealth rests upon Britain because she is the most powerful and wealthy; because as the ex-imperial power all expect assistance from her while having less reason to assume that the other three ought to help them; and because, as the only world power of the four, many other demands are made upon her resources. Canada, for example, could undertake far greater responsibility than at present for aid to the Commonwealth Caribbean. Although she does provide assistance to the West Indies it is nevertheless a very small proportion of the total they receive, the bulk still coming from Britain. Geographic proximity and trading interests make Canada and the West Indies natural partners; thus Canada could well undertake the major aid responsibility for this area and release British resources for use elsewhere.

Similarly, Australia could increase her contribution to Malaysia. In neither instance is it being suggested that Britain is doing too much; if anything, the contrary is the case. Nor that she should 'save' the aid she now gives to these areas. Rather, such a plan demands an increase in total effort by Canada and Australia so that they can undertake these new responsibilities without sacrificing any of their present programmes; while it makes sound administrative and 'interest' sense for them to give high aid priority to areas of closest concern to themselves. In Britain's case her aid effort is too extended and she can always plead in answer to a West Indian request for increased assistance that she has too many other demands upon her resources. If Canada had clearly taken over major Commonwealth responsibility for the West Indies—and in any case was only involved in half a dozen Commonwealth countries altogether—such pleas of too many commitments would be harder to sustain. Moreover, because she had been relieved of certain pressures Britain would be enabled to concentrate more effectively upon other areas. In no sense is this an argument for saying she should do less.

2. Commodity agreements: the economies of many developing countries are dependent upon one or two commodities, often to such an extent that violent fluctuations in world prices for one raw material can ruin the progress made in all other sectors of the economy. Many Commonwealth developing countries are particularly susceptible to this kind of one crop or one raw material dependence: Zambia and copper, the West Indies and sugar, Ghana and cocoa.

The Commonwealth Sugar Agreement has been of real help to sugar-producing countries and does guarantee them some assured income. Even so, the necessity to rely upon a single commodity of this nature can make economic planning especially difficult. Thus, violent fluctuations in world cocoa demands have seriously affected Ghanaian planning. While the Prime Minister of Trinidad could claim that whereas in the early 1950's two and a half tons of sugar were sufficient to purchase a small British car, by 1965 ten tons had to be sold in exchange for the same car. In other words, for years the terms of trade have moved against commodity and raw material producers and in favour of the manufacturing nations.

If a developing country has to rely upon one or two major commodities as its main source of revenue it becomes crucially important for planning purposes that both prices and sales of these products can be reasonably certain. Since so many Commonwealth countries do depend upon commodities, assistance with price support is an obvious method of giving aid. Apart from the Sugar Agreement, however, there has been great reluctance to grant quotas or guarantee prices. Firm quota arrangements—that is, promises to take a minimum quantity of a specific product in any year—could be given by the rich Commonwealth nations to the developing ones dependent upon commodities while agreements as to minimum prices, no matter what the world price, would ensure that reasonable economic planning could take place. Such agreements should be for not less than five years at a time.

The result might mean that Britain pays Ghana far higher prices for its cocoa than any other country—at least up to the agreed quota—

but this would only be another way of providing aid and in Ghanaian terms would guarantee some stability of income so that subsequent economic planning would be that much easier.

3. Provision of markets: one of the difficulties facing many developing countries is that, although aid enables them to build up new industries, trade restrictions—tariffs and other protective measures—often make it impossible for them to sell the goods they produce and so earn the foreign exchange they need. There is little point in Britain providing aid so that Nigeria can start a textile industry if thereafter she will not buy Nigerian textiles.

Now during the 1950's, despite protests from Lancashire, Britain initiated a policy that permitted a considerable influx of cheap Commonwealth textiles, especially from India, Pakistan and Hong Kong, into Britain; the results were twofold: the Commonwealth countries concerned could sell the products of their textile industries in a developed country and earn much-needed sterling; the British industry, in order to survive such competition, was forced to modernize and in fact did so remarkably well. Growing clamour from Lancashire has forced a review and may yet curtail this enlightened policy.

A daring innovation in aid policy aimed at the long-term increase of trade for a developing country and the modernization of an existing industry or indeed the switching to a totally new industry by a developed country could be based upon the textile example quoted above. For a long time to come British industry in overall terms will be technically far superior to that of developing Commonwealth countries. As a deliberate aspect of her aid policy Britain should concentrate upon improving those industries where she has the long-term advantage; and, deliberately, phasing out rather than protecting old industries where Commonwealth competition is catching up. Thus, to keep to the example of textiles (although the principle extends into many other lines—bicycles, simple machinery and so on) Britain should aim over a limited period—say five years—to permit unrestricted entry without duties or quotas of Commonwealth textiles, no matter what this does to her own industry. By adopting such a policy Britain would give to her Commonwealth partners the markets and means of earning the exchange they so desperately need—a far better and more effective way of aiding them than simply making them loans or grants.

Meanwhile, in Britain itself the Government would allocate money that otherwise might have gone in aid for the purpose of retraining the displaced textile workers (in this instance) and starting new, technically more advanced industries in place of those that cheaper competition had forced out of business. Many political objections can be raised to such an approach—they always are—but the end results would be of real value to both donor and recipient. On the one hand Britain would be forced to modernize and concentrate upon industrial advances where she can hold a technical lead while at the same time providing a much-needed market for developing Commonwealth countries—perhaps the most valuable form of aid that a developed country can give; on the other hand developing countries would be able to make maximum gains in fields they are most in a position to tackle.

Such a policy would be politically difficult to implement and open to fierce objections in Britain itself. It amounts to the deliberate phasing out of certain industries in developed countries so as to provide for developing countries markets for the products their own new industries can best produce. But it is not really as one-sided as it might at first appear. It would also have genuine compensations for the donor: it would act as a spur to the technological advance of a country such as Britain. And in the long run it would lead to greater economic interdependence of the Commonwealth.

It is this kind of imaginative and courageous approach to aid problems, one that entails a true partnership of interests between both parties concerned, that could change drastically the whole dependence of poor upon rich countries and begin a proper substitution of trade for aid.

4. A joint approach to aid: continuing and often exaggerated fears of any centralizing tendencies, though possibly justified during the early days of transition from Empire into Commonwealth, are now increasingly a sign of immaturity—backward-looking nationalism— and suggestions of central or joint approaches to problems should no

longer be dismissed so readily. Since the habit of co-operation as well as the means exist in so many areas of Commonwealth activity, reluctance to use such facilities to the full only represents a waste.

The recent establishment of a Commonwealth Secretariat was marred by the suspicious manoeuvring that surrounded it. Instead of Commonwealth countries welcoming what could be a major instrument of closer and more genuinely equal co-operation, they appeared more concerned so to limit the powers of the Secretariat that it is at present little more than an office responsible for arranging details of conferences. Britain, the old Dominions and India were foremost in demonstrating such parochial jealousies and most reluctant to surrender any real power to it. In fact, the Secretariat could be used as a key instrument in developing a common aid policy for the Commonwealth.

As in so many other things the difficulty in evolving a Commonwealth aid policy results chiefly from narrow nationalist fears about surrendering sovereignty. If the Commonwealth as a body could give aid meaning in human terms, recognizing that by almost any standards there is something wrong with a world in which at one end of the scale an Indian is expected to survive an on annual average income of about £25 while at the other a Canadian has more than £700, then progress could be made. In looking for an aid 'aim' (many things are suggested such as bringing the developing countries to the point of 'economic take-off' and so on) a starting point might well be to set a minimum figure—a *per capita* income of not less than £75 per annum—as one all people in the Commonwealth should have to live on; then base long-term aid policies upon assisting the poorer Commonwealth countries to achieve this target.

Should the Commonwealth ever decide upon such a joint approach to aid an effective way to deal with it would be through the Secretariat: or, rather, a branch of the Secretariat could be established as a Commonwealth Aid Council. It would work somewhat like the Colombo Plan but would have greater scope and more real power, above all, finance. All members of the Commonwealth would belong. The Council would be in continual session although it would have a major, full-scale meeting once a year.

K

The first job of the Council would be to have available all possible information about the aid needs of Commonwealth countries and the total sources of capital and personnel that the richer members could provide. At each annual meeting members would declare their most pressing needs: for assistance at government level and for private investment. The rich countries would then state what resources they had made available for aid purposes for that year. A sub-committee representing private enterprise interests could also indicate likely businesses that could be induced to invest in developing Commonwealth members. When the Council had formed a picture of the needs and possible resources to meet them there would follow the more delicate tasκ of deciding upon priorities and how best the Commonwealth's total development resources could be used.

A number of advantages would follow from working in this fashion. First and most crucial—a great psychological advance—the Commonwealth would begin to develop the feeling that it was tackling the problem as a whole: that, for example, the difficulties of Tanzania were something that all could take a pride in solving. Second, the sting—the constant feeling of a superior-inferior relationship between donor and recipient—could be taken out of the process of aid. The Council could make the recipient of aid feel that he had been selected by the whole group for assistance and this would make easier both the acceptance of large aid as well as, where appropriate, some form of supervision of the aid's use. Third, the declaration each year (accompanied by forecasts for the future as well) of the total of assistance available would make it far simpler for the developing countries to plan properly. Too often they have no idea where the next amount of aid will come from or whether they will be able to complete some phase of development that has been started because outside help was forthcoming. Fourth, the group would decide priorities for the use and distribution of the resources at its disposal.

One of the great values of such a scheme would be that it attempts to get over the worst aspects of bilateral aid and introduce a multilateral pattern instead. We have already discussed (see above, pages 110–111) the objections to making all aid multilateral through the United Nations. Though in theory this would be the best way to administer aid, in practice international jealousies make it unlikely that a total channelling of aid through the United Nations would in fact work well, but rather might lead to a diminution of the total effort. But such an approach in the Commonwealth need not fail for the same reasons: just because of the ties that exist and the smaller nature of the group, such an experiment is worth trying.

There are, of course, dangers. If a Commonwealth Aid Council is to decide priorities no doubt some members would complain that their interests were insufficiently regarded by the group as a whole; or that India, for example, then got the lion's share of available resources. But the very relationship existing within the association would act to correct such imbalances. Roughly speaking, priorities ought to be worked out in terms of size and population; national *per capita* income; internal resources; and the existing stage of development. Weighting could be given according to special factors and difficulties such as the inability of very small and poor units to attract outside investment at all and so on. India would certainly head the list; Pakistan and Nigeria would come next; Ceylon, East and Central Africa, Sierra Leone would follow; countries such as Malaysia and Ghana with sectors of the economy highly developed and considerably higher *per capita* incomes than the others would come much lower down the scale; small countries such as Trinidad and Jamaica, with relatively high *per capita* incomes, would nonetheless have their special problems—overpopulation and reliance upon only one or two industries—taken into account. The Council would also allocate some of the resources to dependencies which had not yet received independent status, although the main responsibility for these should still rest with Britain in most cases, with Australia and New Zealand in those for which they are already the responsible authorities. On achieving independence within the Commonwealth a new member would automatically become a part of the Aid Council and be rated according to the accepted priorities. If such a policy could be adopted and the general fairness of its rating be accepted by everyone it would become far easier to turn down a request for assistance than if, as at present, this has to be done on a bilateral basis as between Britain and

Malaysia, for example, leading as it so often does to bad feelings and recriminations between the two countries.

No doubt 'realists' will condemn such a suggested approach as far too utopian, but in fact it is not. Of course there would be many difficulties to overcome, but once such an idea could be accepted in principle the normal habits of Commonwealth co-operation could make it work. The gains from working in such a way would more than compensate for the early difficulties that would certainly have to be faced. The great achievement of such a joint aid effort would be found in the creation of a feeling that problems were common to all and could best be solved by tackling them as a group. As progress was made in dealing with the various problems of individual Commonwealth countries so the task of Commonwealth development could be made into an increasingly exciting joint venture.

Suggestions for an overall Commonwealth policy for aid do not set limits upon the sovereignty of its individual members; rather they represent a mature recognition of a common problem and the search for the best way in which to solve it.

CHAPTER 6

Neo-colonialism

IN KEEPING with the speed of change that has characterized so many of the revolutionary processes that have dominated the world since the Second World War—the revolutions of expectations, of Empires disintegrating, of modernization and industrialization, of political alignments and non-alignments—it only needs a few years for a new aspect of international relations to be accepted as normal practice. In the mid-1950's no one talked of neo-colonialism; by the mid-1960's the phrase has become normal, expected as a description of relations between rich and poor, between old imperial powers and recent colonies now independent.

The term 'neo-colonialism' is used to cover a variety of activities, real or imagined, on the part of the rich industrially developed countries—both Eastern and Western—within the poor developing countries; actions that are considered to be a threat to the true independence of small weak nations and that further the aims and interests of the more powerful. Thus, aid with 'strings'; large-scale private investment involving control of key industries or resources; attempts to maintain military bases in newly independent countries; the advice or behaviour of expatriates: these and many more activities of the governments or representatives of rich countries in the developing world may be branded as neo-colonialist.

More particularly the accusation of neo-colonialist activities has been levelled against the old imperial powers and especially against Britain. In such cases the accusation is based upon several assumptions: that the imperial power only withdrew reluctantly; that it still has many interests in the new state which it desires to further after independence; that, having lost direct political control, it hopes none-theless to continue pushing its own advantage by using new methods; and since, because of the past, it still has great influence in the new state—the laws and institutions it established giving rise to similar patterns of political thought and behaviour; the presence of ex-patriates, possibly settlers as well, and large business interests; the fact that in all likelihood it is the biggest aid donor—all help to con-vince the political leaders of such a new country that the old imperial power does have continuing designs to control the country's destiny.

Thus, whereas before independence, Britain could control what happened in her colonies by direct political decree if need be, after independence she might still attempt to influence and exercise a large measure of control by economic means in particular: aid, investment; trade agreements and concessions; and the presence of expatriates in positions of importance in government. Politicians in weak countries, dependent upon outside aid in one form or another, will often insist that almost any action taken by the past imperial power is neo-colonialist in character. This is hardly the case but there is an element of truth, sometimes substantial, in the accusation. On the other hand, a country such as Britain will deny indignantly that anything it does has neo-colonialist motivations—that all its assistance is purely altru-istic and such accusations are base ingratitude in the face of genuine aid. Such replies are too ingenuous. Bearing in mind the consistent way in which nations always put their own advantage first, then of course a country such as Britain which already possesses a position of influence in a new state (and the old imperial powers have the greatest advantage in this respect, hence the consistency with which they are made the primary targets for charges of neo-colonialism) will use it where possible to further its own objectives. To deny that this hap-pens is nonsense. This does not mean, however, that any offer of aid, any investment, or the behaviour of all expatriates is neo-colonialist. As always, motives are mixed and must be recognized as such.

It is significant that the phrase was first given currency by Nkrumah and grew in importance in direct relation to the number of small territories which have received independence. This is no accident: it reflects the real and continuing need of such territories for outside assistance; their weakness, especially in economic terms; and therefore the degree of opportunity that exists for neo-colonialist practices. When independence was achieved by British India the successor states, India and Pakistan, although economically weak and in need of many kinds of aid, were still too vast and too powerful for there to be any practical opportunities for so-called neo-colonialist activities or manipulations behind the scenes. Consequently, during the decade 1947 to 1957, despite many attempts to pressure them into policies advantageous to the West or the East, the methods used were in an older diplomatic tradition.

Independence throughout most of the African continent, however, produced dozens of new states many with populations averaging only 5 million or less; some unable to stand alone economically, at least for a considerable time; others depending upon large numbers of expatriates for the skills needed to keep government going and to make possible the implementation of their economic plans. Small wonder therefore if the growth of neo-colonialism in practice and imagination has coincided with the achievement of independence by so many relatively small and often economically non-viable units on the African continent.

Now although neo-colonialism is a term covering relations between the rich and strong and the poor and developing on a world scale, it has particular relevance to the Commonwealth and especially in economic terms. In fact, some of the most forthright charges of neo-colonialism have been made against Britain by politicians in African Commonwealth countries. It should not be surprising that this is so: as the greatest of the imperial powers Britain had most opportunities—which she took—to build up her interests—economic or political—in a wide variety of places. After granting independence, not only have these 'interests' she established continued to exist but in many cases her new Commonwealth partners have in fact, despite political freedom, been in continuing need of financial or technical assistance on a big scale and Britain has remained their first source of supply; a large British presence has persisted in the country and the consequent opportunity for neo-colonialist activities and subsequent accusations has been considerable.

COMMONWEALTH AFRICA—1966

1. GHANA. Military coup and the overthrow of President Nkrumah, February 1966.

2. NIGERIA. Military coup January 1966 and the overthrow of the Federal Government (including the death of the Prime Minister, Abubakar Sir Tafawa Balewa); a second military coup in July; then tension between the country's three main regions continued for the rest of the year while they attempted to work out new political relationships with the centre and each other.

3. UGANDA. Deposition of the Kabaka of Uganda by the Prime Minister, Dr. Obote, June 1966.

4. TANZANIA. No diplomatic relations with Britain since the OAU decision of 15 December 1965 at Addis Ababa.

5. RHODESIA. UDI declared on 11 November 1965. Sanctions proving ineffective. Commonwealth leaders meeting at Lagos in January 1966 and in London in September 1966 devoted virtually all their time to the Rhodesia crisis which threatens to split the Commonwealth.

6. BOTSWANA. The former High Commission Territory of Bechuanaland became an independent member of the Commonwealth on 30 September 1966.

7. LESOTHO. The former High Commission Territory of Basutoland became an independent member of the Commonwealth on 4 October 1966.

8. ZAMBIA. As the result of the Rhodesian crisis searching for alternate trade routes and means of supply other than through Rhodesia.

9. SOUTH AFRICA. Not a member of the Commonwealth since 1961 but of predominant political importance to British and Commonwealth countries in Africa: (a) By supplying Rhodesia and refusing to apply sanctions is helping to prolong the Rhodesian crisis. (b) Botswana, Lesotho (entirely surrounded by South African territory) and Swaziland are all heavily dependent economically on South Africa. (c) South Africa's policy of apartheid must eventually lead to major political troubles that are bound to affect Commonwealth African countries. (d) Heavy British investment in and trade with South Africa make the British Government loathe to take strong action against South Africa (even over her tacit support of Rhodesian UDI).

COMMONWEALTH AFRICA - 1966

It is important to understand the reasons for neo-colonialist charges; they are bound up intimately with the process of decolonization. Almost inevitably after a colony becomes independent one of the first psychological needs of its leaders has been to assert, in particular, complete independence from the colonial power; no doubt this is a passing phase but it is an important one. Charges of neo-colonialism are a part of this more general pattern of asserting that a real break has taken place with the imperial power. Thus, both for this reason and because in part at least they are true such charges should cause neither surprise nor shock.

The political facts governing relations between countries should be recognized all the time, not simply when it is convenient to do so. In Commonwealth terms it is no good Britain being upset when leaders of new African states accuse her of neo-colonialism; only if all the highly complex series of motives, relations and links that operate between Commonwealth countries are clearly understood can any sense be made out of possibilities for a continuation of the Commonwealth in the future.

Neo-colonialism is a major factor in relations between rich developed and poor developing Commonwealth countries and most especially between Britain and the developing Commonwealth. It will continue to influence these relations for some time to come, possibly as long as aid for development has to be given. What neo-colonialism represents, therefore, is of great importance; and, as is so often the case, it is less important whether or not charges of neo-colonialism are true than that they are made.

First, what does neo-colonialism mean to developing countries? Above all else it represents their fears. They have recently achieved independence often after a severe and sometimes long-drawn-out political struggle. Naturally enough therefore they resent and suspect any action from outside and most particularly from the old imperial power that appears to threaten the independence they have so recently gained. All too often, moreover, the realization has only come after independence that political control alone is hardly enough; that a country whose economy depends substantially upon outside sources for investment and aid or whose efficient running can only be ensured by the presence of skilled expatriates is to that extent still controlled (or at least capable of being manoeuvred) by such outside powers. In other words, gaining political control may only mean the first and easiest part of a much longer process of becoming truly free. As a result they are only too ready to see in the actions of the powerful—the donor nations—attempts to undermine their new independence. While above all they suspect the erstwhile imperial power of trying to take advantage of their weakness and perpetuate control by more devious 'back seat' methods that it had not found necessary to use when it possessed the political authority.

Such suspicions may be exaggerated but they are not altogether ill-founded. The behaviour of the imperial powers towards their one-time colonies has hardly been of such an impeccable nature as to destroy the validity of such fears; if anything, to the contrary. They have tried consistently and understandably enough to reap maximum advantage from their position: thus, for example, in colony after colony Britain has attempted to maintain a military presence or base of some kind after independence has been granted. Many Commonwealth countries have, at least for a short time, agreed: partly from habit, partly because Britain has made it worth while for them to do so, partly, perhaps, owing to specific local crises. But sooner or later the drawbacks to having a base have come to outweigh the benefits: usually because the country concerned has found itself open to criticism as a 'stooge' of the West, as not maintaining a policy of non-alignment and so on—and Britain has been asked to withdraw. In these cases Britain has relied upon her existing influence, past habit and the economic advantages she could offer as a means of obtaining a particular end that she wanted. In other words, her actions have been classic illustrations of neo-colonialism as politicians of the new states have come to define it. This then is neo-colonialism in action as the developing countries expect it to be applied.

It must also be admitted, however, that neo-colonialism has become a useful label or charge to be employed against an old colonial power for quite different political reasons. Thus, deliberately, new countries wishing to embarrass or condemn the actions of the great powers—because they disagree with their policy or have failed to gain their aims in particular negotiations—will accuse them of neo-colonialism often without justification.

On the other hand, the rich, powerful nations accused of such practices regard neo-colonialism in a totally different light. They resent such charges, partly because they come too near the truth for comfort. Moreover, as the givers of aid and other benefits (at least as they see them) they feel that such accusations are gross ingratitude. Instead of having their assistance warmly appreciated they find it looked upon with suspicion and their motives called into question. Not surprisingly they react bitterly when a weak country they have helped tells them—and the world—that they have only done so for their own advantage, to perpetuate their control behind the scenes and so on. The fact that this is too often true in no sense makes the accusation easier to bear; rather, the vehemence of a denial is often in direct proportion to the degree of truth contained in the charge.

It is pointless for powerful nations to be offended. Just because they are strong they tend to overlook the feelings and susceptibilities of the weak. They should be more ready to recognize that words— charges of this kind—often represent the only weapons that weak countries have to bargain with at all. Thus accusations of neo-colonialism are one way, sometimes the only one, against powers too great for them to handle that small countries can use in order to say: keep out of our internal affairs; or, 'no strings' when dealing with aid offers. These accusations also represent a means of political assertion against the previous imperial power as well as a means of psychological pressure. A charge repeated often enough tends to stick and within narrow limits a country such as Britain does not wish to be branded in this fashion.

Three fields in which charges of neo-colonialism are frequently made and where opportunities for such practices abound are: aid; business investment; and the presence of expatriate technical assistance personnel or advisers.

We have already examined the reasons for aid giving. Here it is only necessary to look briefly at the relations on either side. Thus, a donor, cynical and self-interested though his motives may be, does expect at least a show of gratitude. Moreover, rich countries have to meet many other calls upon limited resources and justify aid in political terms at home. Further, should there be clear mismanagement of the aid given, instances of corruption or little apparent progress as a result, then, both a natural desire to see its resources properly used as well as political demands for tighter control of taxpayers' money will act to persuade a donor nation to demand more say in the use of its aid: in other words, 'strings'.

All these factors operate anyway most of the time and present enough problems of their own for a donor to face. They will be greatly exacerbated if a recipient of aid levels charges of neo-colonialism against the donor and, instead of making the task of aid giving easier and more pleasant by a suitable response in terms of 'good' behaviour, compliance with the donor's wishes and gratitude, makes it harder by harsh words, doubting the donor's motives, accusing him of exploitation and so on. In the circumstances it is not surprising that periodically various political elements in aid-giving nations adopt an attitude either of 'toughness' —'we shall only give aid on precise conditions that render us a return'—or of disinterest— 'why should we continue to help these people at all?'

On the other side the recipients, the weaker members in the aid-giving relationship, find themselves in an unenviable position from which there is often no escape. Their needs are great, sometimes desperate; the political demands of their people for progress not to be denied; their fear of exploitation usually has a firm enough foundation in their past history; while their determination to maintain their recently acquired independence, their pride and dislike of having to rely upon aid of any kind all combine to make them deeply suspicious of any offers of assistance. Moreover, the history of aid, its use especially in the early years as a Cold War weapon; the fact that small countries approaching independence, with little enough apparently of economic or political value to offer, suddenly find a host of great powers falling over each other to establish embassies and vying with one another in their offers of assistance; or past cases of aid having been given with 'strings' too obviously attached; of aid offers being conditional upon the acceptance of other quite different terms or relations being entered into; as well as a clear understanding of the various motives prompting rich nations to give aid at all—all this only serves to ensure that recipients, while accepting aid, retain a healthy cynicism about the apparently generous reasons for it.

Consequently recipient countries are determined to avoid all 'strings' if they can; they will ruthlessly and justifiably, from their point of view, play one donor off against another; and wherever donors appear to reap too many advantages from the assistance they give, the natural reaction—and sometimes the only available weapon —is the accusation of neo-colonialism.

But perhaps most important of all reasons for the attacks made upon the old imperial powers is simply that of national pride. The realization that despite independence they are still so dependent upon their old colonial masters can be very bitter; as much as anything charges of neo-colonialism reflect the feeling of impotence that such dependence must carry with it.

In the field of business, conditions may be slightly different; the reasons for accusations of neo-colonialism are the same: dependence and pride. In any case the economic position of a developing country is sufficiently difficult: it has few enough industries upon which to base its prosperity and may well have to rely almost entirely upon one or two raw materials. Such a narrow economic base presents any government with a large number of problems. If, in addition, the major industry is controlled by an expatriate company or the main resource is mined or extracted by one the consequent frustrations may be almost unbearable. Considerations such as these led the Iranian Government to force the Abadan (Persian oil) crisis of the early 1950's and insist that Iran should at least have a part share in the one great resource the country possessed. Similarly, the recent history of British Guiana has been at least as much one of nationalist attitudes of antagonism towards the giant firm of Bookers that controls so much of the economy as it has been towards the colonial government.

In circumstances of this nature if a developing country wishes to expand a product or open up a new industry it finds itself obliged to approach expatriate capital and expertise and ask if they will do the job, since it does not possess the resources on its own. Thus 90% of

Zambia's wealth lies in copper controlled by two expatriate companies; 80% of Guyana's wealth—sugar and commerce and bauxite—is controlled by London and Montreal based companies; while again and again in other developing countries the same kind of dependence upon outside business interests exists. When the occasional outcries in Britain about American money buying into key British industries or the more serious Canadian fears of being an economic satellite of the United States are remembered, then, the only surprising aspect of neo-colonialist charges levelled against expatriate business in developing countries is that they are not made more often.

Furthermore, business interests are not notably forward in lessening possibilities of friction. They devote far too much attention to fears of expropriation, basing them upon a ridiculously small number of examples, while saying little or nothing about the vast majority of cases where their investments in the developing world have been welcome, profitable and without political troubles. They ask for guarantees for their investment; they often act as though equal powers with the governments of the countries in which they operate; then appear shocked when in return unpleasant things are said of them.

The presence of large numbers of expatriate technical assistance personnel or advisers in developing countries is bound to be a source of friction. In the first place the fact that they are there at all acts as a constant reminder to the country they are helping that it needs them; that its own people are not yet able to do the jobs; that it has not yet got enough trained personnel. Second, and often particularly true of British aid, many of her technical assistance personnel are previous colonial officers and no matter how they have tried to readjust to new conditions, all too often they take with them attitudes from the past: that the people they are helping are not yet ready for independence and that their presence bears this fact out; that things were managed better under the old colonial régime and standards are now falling; while, as advisers, they tend to think in terms of older colonial patterns which put law and order first rather than in new ways which give priority to progress and development. They talk of 'maintaining standards' and mean their British standards whether these are applicable to the country in which they serve or not. Such people may be necessary for the time being and a country's immediate progress may have to depend upon their presence; sometimes they may even be right in the criticisms they make. But none of these facts mean that they are wanted except in the negative sense that the country cannot do without them; positively when such technical assistance experts have left and the country can manage without them, only then will it feel that it is nearer to a state of true independence.

It has been a theme of this book that most Commonwealth links, certainly the economic ones, are based upon concepts of advantage. 'Neo-colonialism' really represents no more than a recognition of facts: on the one hand that the many ways in which a rich country such as Britain is involved in the affairs of its poorer Commonwealth partners is only because it is to her advantage that it should be so; and on the other hand that these poorer countries must continue to be dependent upon British aid, investment and technical assistance for a long time to come, whether they like it or not.

With all the exaggerations that are used on both sides, the term neo-colonialism nonetheless does describe part of the relationship existing between the rich and the developing nations; if Britain can continue to maintain its interests in countries which were once its colonies by using 'neo-colonial' methods then, of course, it will do so. Now this is no more than a fact of international behaviour. In Commonwealth terms what matters is that the whole series of relationships covered by the term neo-colonialism should be clearly understood. Basically, this is a question of attitudes: on the part of the developing countries making the accusations—these represent frustrations arising out of their dependence, usually upon Britain; while, in Britain, reactions to such charges, though sometimes understandable, are often a means of expressing resentment at the loss of Empire.

Neo-colonialism (or whatever term may be used) will continue as long as aid is given or weak and developing countries are obliged to look to more powerful and wealthy ones for assistance. It is an inevitable part of such a relationship. But more than this, neo-

colonialism represents the second stage in the process of decolonization: first comes the actual achievement of independence; then,
following the realization that political freedom does not necessarily
mean economic freedom, the resultant fear of continuing control by
the imperial power now using different methods naturally leads to
charges of neo-colonialism.

Sometimes these charges are justified; sometimes they are not, but
whichever may be the case the fears are there and that is enough to
produce the accusations. Neo-colonialism will remain an important
factor in international relations for the foreseeable future. It will
become less important when one-time colonies have enjoyed independent status for a sufficiently long time that their fears of continuing control from the imperial power die out, to be replaced by a more
healthy two-way understanding. It will diminish still more as a factor
when aid has begun to achieve proper successes, not in the present
sense of 'holding operations' that simply enable countries to survive,
but by bringing recipients to the point of economic take-off so that
the need for aid begins to disappear. This is still a long way in the
future.

Meanwhile an honest recognition of the causes behind the different
charges of neo-colonialism is the first step towards eradicating or at
least mitigating their worst effects. Here the onus for action must rest
with the more powerful donor nations, Britain especially in the
Commonwealth, since neo-colonialism is the result of suspicions and
fears as to their motives by the dependent, less powerful countries.
Neo-colonialism must be accepted as the expression of complications
which are bound to accompany any one-sided relationship between
rich and poor or strong and weak. In the Commonwealth it affects all
aspects of economic co-operation between the developed and developing members: aid, investment, trade agreements, the presence of
expatriate technical assistance personnel, military bases and the
dependence of the one group of countries upon the other. Most of all
it affects the relations existing between Britain and her past colonies
since, in part, it is a stage in the whole process of decolonization by
Britain and of genuinely achieving true independence, in spirit as
well as in name, by her past colonies.

L

CHAPTER 7

Immigration and Minorities

BRITONS emigrating overseas have long been considered one of the vital links of Empire; while in the modern Commonwealth era the presence in the old Dominions of populations composed predominantly of British stock has been a key factor in maintaining the 'family' aspect of the group. Appeals to a common heritage of ideas, institutions, laws and ways of life have been reinforced by more emotional references to 'home' on the part of Australians, New Zealanders or Canadians; to 'kith and kin' across the seas—in fact, a whole folklore based upon racial affinities. But sentiments such as these have only followed settlement based upon quite different economic and political considerations.

Britain's first North American colonies were founded by men whose primary motives were either straightforward gain or a desire to escape political and religious restrictions at home and found communities in which they could behave as they wished—certainly in another way from that prevailing in England. Often their concern was less with the links binding them to the 'mother' country than with a wish to sever such bonds and start anew. Only when threatened—by the French or Spanish, or by the natives—did they suddenly and loudly recall kinship with England and expect her protection. Then such sentiments, reinforced by political considerations of power and economic advantage, would usually galvanize England into action which often led in its turn to further imperial expansion.

It was the imperialism of the late nineteenth century—Kipling expounding his creed of the 'white man's burden', Joseph Chamberlain preaching his conviction that Britain had a responsibility to spread

Anglo-Saxon culture and rule to as many parts of the world as possible—that gave currency to the largely twentieth-century idea of a 'family of nations'. Loyalty to Britain in two world wars by the old Dominions—and the Afrikaner opposition to fighting Britain's battles, especially in the 1939–1945 war, only emphasized the bonds between the mother country and emigrants of British stock—helped maintain the idea for a time. Yet today, if anything, emphasis upon British solidarity with the white members of the Commonwealth tends to act as a divisive influence in a multiracial Commonwealth a majority of whose members are non-white. This is brought home all the more sharply by the fact that the white Commonwealth countries are also its rich members. The idea of the rich white members 'ganging up' on the remainder has only been averted by the more independent and farsighted statesmanship of Canada which in three crises—Suez, the expulsion of South Africa and, most recently, UDI—has refused to align herself with Britain, Australia and New Zealand.

No doubt kinship is a fine sentiment and as long as Britain was powerful enough to protect the interests of white settlers in Africa or guard Australia and New Zealand in their South Seas isolation, the bond of race could be relied upon as a powerful emotional link. But declining British power and growing economic and political independence by the old Dominions has caused them increasingly to look elsewhere in pursuit of their interests.

Historically, the drain of emigrants to various parts of the Empire has met more usually with opposition in Britain which wanted trade rather than settlements. Far from thinking that their American colonies were spreading English influence seventeenth-century Englishmen regarded them as prejudicial to the country's interests. In the eighteenth century the drain of people was considered as a loss of economic and military power. While for long in the nineteenth century, despite the efforts of men like Gibbon Wakefield to organize planned emigration to the colonies, Australia was looked upon primarily as a dumping ground for the British criminal classes.

Although the idea of emigration as a basis of imperial strength gained ground from the time of Gibbon Wakefield to the end of the nineteenth century, perhaps the most telling commentary upon the whole subject is to be found in the figures for emigrants from Britain in the twenty years 1884–1903, the heyday of imperialism. In every one of those years except the last (1903) more than 50% of all British emigrants went to the United States. Nothing demonstrates more clearly the economic basis of population movements: America presented the greatest opportunities for the future and to America in overwhelming numbers the emigrants went.

As in so much of imperial history emigration was based primarily upon economic considerations. And though other reasons—ridding late Elizabethan England of its 'swarms of pestilential vagabonds'; escaping religious intolerance in the seventeenth century; finding a convenient and distant home for convicts in the nineteenth century; or running from what they believed to be the beginnings of a socialist society they could not stomach in the late 1940's—have all contributed to the general flow, normally it has been the economic push out of Britain, unemployment, overcrowding, the search for markets and new areas for exploitation or the economic pull of greater opportunities offered by Canada, Australia or Africa that have dominated imperial and Commonwealth population movements.

Thus bad times in Britain, whether periods of economic depression or political uncertainty (1957, the year after Suez, saw record numbers of Britons emigrate to Canada and Australia) have led to large outward movements of British emigrants. The old Dominions—Canada and Australia with their vast size and apparent opportunities in particular, but South Africa and New Zealand also—have always needed and usually preferred (South Africa excepted) to have British immigrants rather than any others. In reverse the Dominions of settlement have acted as economic magnets for British settlers: this was especially true during the 1950's when a steady stream of Britons flowed to Canada and Australia; and to Central Africa where the boom in copper and the apparently bright economic future of the Federation attracted many seeking immediate and rapid improvement of their economic condition. Yet to argue that Commonwealth links have played more than a peripheral part in controlling this flow would be naïve. Of course, Britons who decide to emigrate consider the advantages of living with English-speaking people in

countries with similar customs that are in the Commonwealth—
sentiment is important; but this has never diminished the flow to the
United States; nor, since South Africa left the Commonwealth in
1961 has it affected what, if anything, has become an increase of
British numbers going there. Few emigrants to Central Africa since
1945 could claim to be pioneers in the old imperial sense; most went
because of the high standards of living earlier pioneer efforts had
already achieved. While Australia, excepting New Zealand the most
pro-British of Commonwealth countries, whose economy demanded
a rapid expansion of numbers, could only compete with other, more
attractive immigrant countries by offering most generous aid to
'would-be' settlers with its assisted passage scheme. As usual,
economic or other advantages, this time for the individual, have pre-
dominated in guiding his choice of an immigrant country. Commonwealth links, though important, have hardly been decisive.

Whatever the motives for emigration, the advantages to Britain in
particular and in a more general Commonwealth context have been
extensive: the growth of 'family' links; the extension of natural
markets for British goods; loyalty in times of crisis—all have contributed to a tradition that emigrating Britons go to Commonwealth
countries. But there are disadvantages too. In the early days, the
American War of Independence proved this only too clearly: colonies
of settlement were determined to create societies of their own choice,
not simply overseas appendages of Britain. In recent years there has
been a gathering British feeling once again that emigrants represent
an economic loss; this feeling has been reinforced by the 'brain drain'
although the leading 'villain' here has been the United States rather
than Commonwealth countries, while UDI in Rhodesia has shown
how small a chance loyalty stands when measured against self-interest.

Throughout the history of the Empire and often explosively in the
modern Commonwealth movements of people have proved to be both
important and sometimes essential as binding forces and also to be
responsible for the creation of many problems. Because in the 1960's
world racial issues as between white and black have come to play so
prominent a part in the news and the problems of white minorities in

Africa—the Kenya settlers during Mau Mau and before independence; apartheid in South Africa; and, especially in 1966 the Rhodesia
rebellion—have come to threaten the multiracial character of the
Commonwealth, they have tended to obscure non-white problems
relating to immigration and minorities in the Commonwealth as a
whole. Despite Britain's pre-eminence as an exporter of people other
Commonwealth races have not been backward in their tendency to
emigrate. Indians especially have spread to many parts of the
Commonwealth, while from outside its membership the Chinese, a
great migratory people, have supplied minority groups of major
influence in Malaysia (they are the majority in Singapore) and from
time to time, of at least passing political significance in other areas—
Australia and the West Indies, for example.

The Commonwealth is a multiracial society but not solely because
of the different races which form each state. Far more complicated
than this is the internal composition of the individual member states:
mixtures of two or more races, minority groups and the fears and
jealousies to which they give rise. During the 1960's immigration of
coloured Commonwealth citizens into Britain developed into a major
political issue. Antagonisms between Malays and Chinese threaten
the future of Malaysia. White minorities in Africa (and the ever-
present consciousness of South Africa's apartheid) may yet wreck the
Commonwealth multiracial concept. African resentment of Indian
minorities provides another case of strain. The movements of Africans themselves from one country to another though at present not a
serious cause of friction may become one. Similarities as between one
West Indian island and another have not prevented fierce jealousies
from keeping migration between them to little more than a trickle,
while scholarship and training aid by rich Commonwealth countries,
especially Britain, has in recent years given rise to the new problem
of a 'brain drain' of skilled people who remain behind after receiving
training—a loss their own countries can ill afford.

Throughout history minorities have been the focus of national
hatreds; no brave twentieth-century talk of 'one world' has altered
this fact. The economics of Empire have taken Britons, Indians,
Chinese, and, more recently, West Indians and Africans to many parts

of the Commonwealth. In some places—Canada and Australasia—the immigrant represents the majority; in others he has established a minority, sometimes a very powerful one, and in consequence faces the country of his adoption with some of its most difficult and explosive problems. If the Commonwealth is to retain its multiracial character and survive it needs to deal with these problems with more courage and tolerance than it has always been prepared to show.

Commonwealth links are sufficiently tenuous as it is while the problems it faces threaten often enough to break the association apart. With the achievement of independence by all major British colonies, immigration has become a matter for careful controls. Whereas in imperial days the movement of people was primarily under the control of the Colonial Office, now each Commonwealth country, only too aware of racial difficulties, keeps strict watch over any immigration, whether from the Commonwealth or not. By the time the modern Commonwealth had appeared minority problems, some acute and dangerous, existed in many member countries and it is most probable that, should the association break up, it will do so on some racial issue.

Racial problems may differ greatly from one part of the Commonwealth to another but their basis is always the same: fear. It comes out in different ways: the economic fear of losing jobs to invading immigrants with lower living standards; fear of political domination by a more advanced minority group over the indigenous and more backward majority; or, in countries such as Malaysia and Guyana where racial groups are fairly evenly balanced, a combination of the two kinds of suspicion may act to exacerbate more general differences of outlook to produce situations of alternate bitterness and uneasy truce.

No understanding of the Commonwealth—of its prospects for future co-operation or of the economic and racial factors that operate so powerfully in all countries where people have mixed—can be achieved without some examination of immigration policies and minority questions.

Whatever the reasons Britain has long been a major emigrant country and her people have established a tradition for colonization and settlement in many remote parts of the world. With the end of imperial expansion she has continued to supply emigrants who in return helped forge links with 'home' that have played a varied but always important part in the Commonwealth's history. Further, Britain developed the habit of regarding Empire and Commonwealth citizens as also citizens of Britain. Such an attitude was not hard to maintain as long as the flow of people into Britain was on a small scale. After the Second World War two things happened to alter the habit and practice: for economic reasons Britain wished to conserve her population rather than lose it, even to countries such as Australia and Canada. Churchill's post-war speech in which he referred to emigrants as 'rats leaving the sinking ship' signalled, flamboyantly as usual, a change of attitude. Increasingly since then, although Britain has made no move to restrict the free movement of her citizens she has tended to hold the older view that numbers represent economic strength. This has been reinforced both by fears of the 'brain drain', particularly to the United States, and by the need for a large home market to help compete with the giant trading blocs such as Europe.

Despite greater reluctance to see her citizens depart they still continued to emigrate in large numbers for most of the years following the Second World War—to Canada, Australia and South Africa especially and, at least in the boom years of the 1950's to the Rhodesias. Over the same period, however, an increasing flow of Commonwealth citizens backwards from Australia and New Zealand and to a lesser extent from Canada helped compensate Britain for its manpower losses. But though in terms of white emigrants British manpower losses have been partially replaced by an inflow from the old Dominions, the real problem has arisen over the influx into Britain of coloured immigrants.

The British image in race relations is of fundamental importance to any multiracial concept. For many years it stood high and the British people were assumed to be basically tolerant. But problems regarded at a distance are one thing; when close to home they change rapidly. Throughout the 1950's Britain could boast proudly that any Commonwealth citizen could settle in the country and enjoy equal rights with British citizens. The growth of a coloured minority in

Britain, however, has illustrated only too well how principles in the abstract give way to more selfish considerations in practice. The story of coloured immigration into Britain between 1948 and 1965 is instructive, showing only too clearly the highly emotional nature of the racial issue as it affects the whole Commonwealth.

Poverty and overpopulation in the West Indies led to the search for an outlet. The first sailing of the *Empire Windrush* from Jamaica to Britain in 1948 bringing with it some 400 immigrants started an ever-growing stream of West Indians. Later, Cypriots, Indians, Pakistanis and Maltese also took advantage of Britain's 'open door' policy and came seeking the greater opportunities for work that Britain offered. Many were very poor with few skills and little education. Yet despite predictions that they could not be absorbed, not only have the vast majority been fitted into British life without difficulty, but some services in particular—London hospitals relying upon West Indian nurses, the Health Service in North-East England dependent upon Indian and Pakistani doctors, London transport, sectors of the textile industry and so on—would be hard put to survive without a continuing supply of such immigrants. Arguments that coloured immigrants caused problems—of education and housing; of language; by putting too much strain on overworked social services; or that they created coloured ghettoes in places like Brixton, Birmingham and Nottingham—were soon advanced as a reason to limit the flow. Any scale of immigration leads to difficulties, yet the contribution, economic and social, that these newcomers make to British life far outweighs the problems accompanying their presence. Nonetheless, a growing campaign based on economic fears (mainly groundless) and racial intolerance gathered strength during the late 1950's—assisted by the race riots that erupted at Nottingham and Notting Hill Gate at the end of the 1950's which shocked not only Britain but the world—and the old complacency about British tolerance was shattered. Thereafter demands for restrictions grew rapidly. In 1962 the Tory party, then in power, passed the Commonwealth Immigration Act and departed from the principle of free entry; the flow of Commonwealth immigrants to Britain was to be restricted. Although the arguments advanced in favour of the Act were all in economic terms about Britain's limited ability to absorb new numbers and the need for skilled people only, they made little sense. First because the outflow of British emigrants equalled the influx; second because no limit was placed upon the Irish who in fact supplied the greatest number of non-skilled immigrants coming into the country. Racial intolerance, however disguised, was the main reason for the Act. At the time the Socialists in opposition condemned the Act and promised to repeal it when they came to power. During the 1964 election the defeat of Gordon Walker at Smethwick again shocked the world and further tarnished Britain's racial image. The Socialists had second thoughts and in 1965, when in office, they forgot their promise to repeal the 1962 Act; instead they tightened it still further, once more using economic arguments to justify their conduct. Yet at the same time that they were restricting immigrants on economic grounds the new National Plan for Development predicted that by 1970 the labour force would suffer from an overall shortage of 300,000.

Thus, due to mounting pressures, first the Tories in 1962 and then the Socialists in 1965 abandoned their past principles and introduced legislation clearly based upon considerations of race. Both parties made special exceptions to demonstrate their liberalism: the Tories of the Irish, the Socialists of the Maltese. It would have been more to the point if either or both had been prepared to make out a special case for West Indians, surely in greater need of Britain's bounty than either of the other two. Recent British attitudes towards Commonwealth coloured immigrants are immensely important: although economically they are needed and can be absorbed—and some sectors of the economy find it difficult to function efficiently without them (London Transport has a recruitment centre in Barbados); though their contribution more than compensates for the burden they place upon British social services; and despite the National Plan prediction of an overall shortage of labour by 1970, Commonwealth immigrants have been drastically restricted because of racial prejudices. In this case not only have economic considerations but concepts of a multiracial society as well been sacrificed in order to gratify narrowly based arguments of racial intolerance. Such a British lead does not augur well for the future of a multiracial Commonwealth. But if Britain, faced with a serious minority problem for the first time, has reacted in selfish and shortsighted fashion, few of her Commonwealth partners can claim better records.

As a land of vast size with great resources awaiting development Canada has always been an immigrant country, and though the normal fluctuation of economic forces has sometimes meant difficulty when too many newcomers have sought entry (at various times English immigrants seeking jobs in Canada have been met with notices saying 'No Englishmen need apply') more usually the rapidly expanding economy has absorbed all the people it can get. But Canadian immigration policy has always been highly selective: Britons and Frenchmen have had little trouble gaining entry; for others strict quotas have been applied. Though never explicitly stated Canada's policy has always aimed at recruiting white immigrants only. Pressure from India during the 1930's led Mackenzie King to indulge in more than usually tortuous political manoeuvring: the result, Indians in theory could emigrate to Canada, in practice it was impossible. After Indian independence in 1947, however, and following strong pressures from the new Asian members of the Commonwealth, Canada relaxed her laws in 1951 to allow 150 Indians, 100 Pakistanis and 50 Ceylonese a year into the country provided they were sponsored by relatives already there: a very minor concession. Under growing Commonwealth pressure towards the end of the 1950's she further relaxed her laws to permit entry to small numbers of West Indians. This move coincided with a growing Canadian involvement in aid to the Caribbean. But such sudden generosity of Canadian policy towards the West Indies is more apparent than real: with a few special exceptions—students, compassionate cases, and women prepared to work as domestics—strict quotas are applied to the different territories and only people with selected skills are admitted. The effect is not to ease West Indian problems of over-population but rather to cream off skilled people the islands can least afford to lose. Canada could absorb large numbers of coloured immigrants; her patent unwillingness even to take very small numbers once more demonstrates the difficulty of the racial issue.

Like Canada, Australia and New Zealand have based their immigration policies upon unlimited entry for Britons, strict control for most others. Both in fact have sought whites only. The 'White Australia Policy' at least has the merit of honesty if little else: isolated as a white island, cut off from the remainder of the white world by the huge coloured populations to its north and for long fearful of the 'yellow peril' from China and Japan, Australia has rigidly excluded coloured immigrants. With a vast continent to develop and unable to attract all the white settlers she needs this hardly makes economic sense. In Commonwealth terms since, apart from New Zealand, her nearest Commonwealth neighbours are India, Pakistan, Ceylon and Malaysia, it is an insult to the multiracial principle, while in a wider political sense to continue denying entry to coloured immigrants from her north to the vast half-empty stretches of continental Australia represents a blind refusal to recognize facts of geography.

Now the recent changes of British approach to coloured immigration and the longer-standing policies pursued by the old white Dominions are based upon similar fears, partly racial, partly economic. The racial fear is the product of ignorance and prejudice, summed up by such phrases as: they are different, they are dirty, we do not want intermarriage, and so on. Only greater understanding and tolerance will overcome such fears, if at all; in a world that communications are rapidly shrinking into a single community while population explosion is even more rapidly overcrowding it, the sooner such prejudices are faced and overcome the better. The economic fear is based upon the supposition that 'open door' policies would lead to huge influxes of cheap coloured labour that would cause massive unemployment and debase the high living standards these countries now enjoy. But this is largely a fallacy. Immigration is itself controlled by movements of economic expansion and contraction and only when circumstances have been right—and boom conditions existed—has large-scale immigration taken place. Emigrants do not go to new countries where no opportunities exist for them.

Problems arising out of white and coloured contact resulting from immigration affect several African Commonwealth countries—

Kenya, Zambia and Rhodesia in particular—but here the position is reversed and the white settlers form the minority groups. The difficulty in these cases is that of minority *élites*: their high living standards are a cause of resentment to the black majorities, while the key economic positions they hold and the skills they possess make them essential to the progress of these countries. The Mau Mau crisis in Kenya, mainly concerned with Kikuyu land hunger and claims for the 'white highlands', focused attention upon the enormous disparities between black and white living conditions. For some years before independence it was touch and go whether the white minority would come to terms with black majority rule. Luckily they did and Kenya has embarked upon a genuine attempt to be a multi-racial society. Even so, of political necessity, the government has followed a policy of Africanizing jobs of all kinds formerly held by Europeans and the eventual position of the white settlers is far from certain. Many holding more extreme racial views left the country at independence.

Independent Zambia under very difficult conditions complicated by the unhappy legacies of Federation and then the UDI crisis has also followed a determined policy of multiracialism. But in her case circumstances have been different: unlike Kenya, most of whose settlers were farmers, the bulk of Europeans in Zambia are concentrated upon the Copperbelt. The white mining community, drawn almost equally from Britain on the one hand, Rhodesia and South Africa on the other, tend to extremes in their racial views: they went to Zambia on a more or less temporary basis to make good money in the mines rather than as pioneers. But accelerated Zambianization of all but the top technical posts means that by the early 1970's the bulk of these miners will have left while only Europeans with special skills or who genuinely want to make the country their home will remain.

Whether these white minorities in either Kenya or Zambia—as well as the far smaller ones in Tanzania, Malawi and so on—will be able to remain in Africa as accepted and equal members of their societies (indeed, whether these countries will continue in their attempts to remain multiracial) must depend—as so much else in Africa does—upon the eventual outcome of the crisis in Rhodesia.

In this British colony, with a proportionately far larger white minority, the settlers have refused to come to terms with the prospect of black majority rule. Instead, they have illegally seized power in the apparent hope of forestalling indefinitely the day when their position as a privileged ruling *élite* must disappear. This is not the place for a lengthy examination of the Rhodesia question. But one thing is certain. If Britain does not achieve a solution that guarantees eventual majority rule, then the almost inevitable result will be that the subsequent tensions between Africans and Europeans throughout the continent will make the position of all white minorities north of Rhodesia increasingly difficult and finally untenable. The present attempts at multiracial societies will end in failure and this could only be a tragedy for both black and white.

Although African racial issues are dominated by problems relating to the white minorities and always overshadowed by apartheid in South Africa, this does not mean that other tensions and problems do not exist. The contrary is the case. The revolution in Zanzibar a few months after independence was basically racial in character, because, in effect, Britain handed over power to the Arab minority. Considerable numbers of Indian immigrants have settled in East Africa over the years and become entrenched as a commercial middle class of shopkeepers. There are increasing signs in Kenya and elsewhere that their presence is resented: multiracialism in these countries is not simply a matter of coming to terms with the remaining white settlers but also one of accepting the Indian minorities. This as yet is by no means certain. Beyond this looms the question of African acceptance of other African migrants.

The nature of colonial boundaries and the fact that many tribes overlap one or more countries has always meant easy movements across borders: in search of work, to traditional grazing grounds and so on. The long-standing border dispute between Kenya and Somalia is a case in point. Following independence, the rapid growth of parochial nationalism, coupled with the political need for the new leaders to achieve full employment for their own people, threatens more permissive attitudes from the past. Africans from Malawi who have traditionally sought work in the neighbouring countries of

Zambia and Rhodesia may discover increasing barriers—because jobs are reserved for local people. For similar reasons in East Africa the governments of Kenya, Uganda and Tanzania may impose greater restrictions upon the free movement across the borders of their citizens seeking work.

Despite Pan-African sentiments and apparent solidarity over South Africa the lot of South African refugees seeking work in the countries to the north is rapidly becoming more difficult. South African Africans are often better educated than those elsewhere on the continent; moreover, they sometimes appear arrogant. Nonetheless, where possible, they ought to be offered jobs; in fact there have been instances where highly qualified South Africans have been turned down in favour of expatriate Europeans costing twice as much to employ. Thus racial or national prejudice on the African continent is far from confined solely to the question of black and white relations.

Indian emigrants are to be found in many parts of the world and substantial Indian minorities have settled in a number of Commonwealth countries. Apart from the recent influx into Britain they are to be found in Malaysia, East and Central Africa and the West Indies. We have already discussed their position in Africa; it is hardly easy. Indeed, right at the beginning of the twentieth century Gandhi first came to prominence working to improve conditions for Indians who had originally gone to South Africa as indentured labourers. In Malaysia the Indian minority is acceptable to the Malays as a further counterbalance to the far greater numbers of Chinese. But in the West Indies, British Guiana (recently independent as Guyana) has for years faced communal difficulties, sometimes resulting in strife, because of her racial divisions: approximately 50% of the population are Indian (largely descended from indentured labour brought in to work the sugar plantations at the turn of the century); the balance are composed of 40% of African descent, while the remainder are made up of Amerindians, Portuguese, Chinese and Europeans. In order to satisfy the fears of the rest of the population that independence would not mean permanent political control by the Indians Britain worked out a system of proportional representation instead of handing over power to a simple majority system as she did throughout the rest of the Empire.

The West Indies are one of the few Commonwealth areas that can truly claim to be multiracial; centuries of mixing and intermarriage have produced every gradation of colour and to an outsider it is hard to differentiate between say a Jamaican and a Barbadian. In theory there ought to be few difficulties about inter-island immigration. In practice parochialism and jealousies have precluded any major movement of people between the various parts of the West Indies. A special point of dispute for the ill-fated West Indian Federation was over the question of emigration between the islands. Of all the Caribbean territories British Honduras on the mainland is under-populated and needs relatively many more people if it is to progress economically. Yet, at a time when Jamaica is desperately seeking outlets for its surplus population, British Honduras is loathe to admit them as immigrants because she fears that the more go-ahead Jamaicans would soon come to dominate her economy.

One other racial group forming minorities in several Common-wealth countries is the Chinese. Industrious and acute business men, they tend to form tight communities and dominate commercial enterprise. Only in Malaysia do their numbers and economic strength present a major problem: the secession of Singapore from the Federation was due to the predominantly Chinese character of its population and Malayan fears of their economic and political power. Chinese 'coolies' in nineteenth-century Australia gave rise to the scares of the 'yellow peril' and were the original cause of the 'White Australia Policy'.

One other aspect of Commonwealth immigration concerns students. Large numbers of coloured Commonwealth students, especially Africans, arrive every year in the rich Commonwealth countries, and most of all in Britain where they currently number more than 45,000. After completing their studies at least some stay on, allured by the greater economic opportunities offered by a country like Britain or reluctant to return to more spartan conditions in their own countries. Unfortunately, these represent a disastrous 'brain drain' from developing Commonwealth countries. The fact that they have gone overseas to study indicates that they are *élite* material and Commonwealth African countries, for example, can ill afford to lose any people who have acquired skilled training. The numbers involved are small but in terms of abilities those who do not return home represent a considerable economic loss.

In summary, immigration policies and the position of minorities present the Commonwealth with some of its most difficult problems. Economic forces—overpopulation or unemployment in an emigrant country—the need for people and economic booms in immigrant countries, as well as earlier pioneer schemes of settlement in Africa, have created the patterns that now exist. But because racial relationships—the most difficult and touchy of all—are involved, economic needs such as Britain's projected labour shortage in 1970 or Canada's absolute and continuing need for an expanding population will always be subordinated to political considerations of controlling minorities.

Multiracial principles quickly collapse when faced by the fears that accompany differences in colour and race. If a multiracial Commonwealth is to survive it must make more determined efforts to overcome such prejudices than it has managed to do so far. Certainly there are some bright spots and valiant attempts at integration are taking place in many countries; but, too often, suspicions and resentments, intolerance and lack of understanding predominate. Rhodesia alone may yet wreck the Commonwealth. The explosion of the world's population and the shrinking of frontiers make future policies based upon tight racial enclaves practically unrealistic and ideally repugnant. Whether racial purists like it or not the increasing movement of people across borders, the overspill from densely populated areas into underpopulated ones must form an inevitable and growing aspect of future international relations. Either this can be recognized as a fact, in which case there is time to plan for peaceful and growing integration of peoples; or it can be ignored and resisted until economic necessity forces the overcrowded countries of South-East Asia, for example, to spill over into sparsely populated Australia and so on.

Apart from war there is no greater issue facing the world than that of relations between the different races and particularly between the

M

rich white ones and the coloured remainder. The outlook at present is gloomy, while the urgency of the problem is grossly underrated. Should the illegal régime in Rhodesia be allowed to get away with UDI this could signify the beginning of a world split permanently along lines of colour. There could hardly be a greater disaster.

It is in this context that the position of the Commonwealth is so important. With all its imperfections it does represent the only genuine attempt at a multiracial approach to problems existing among a particular group of nations. If, with all the multiracial advantages the association possesses and the habit of co-operation it has managed to establish in a wide number of fields, it fails to tackle racial differences successfully, there is little hope that any other group of nations will succeed. But to make a valid contribution, all the problems presented by immigration policies and by minority groups must be re-examined and tackled jointly. Despite all the arguments advanced to justify the reversal of her 'open door' Commonwealth immigration policy, Britain was wrong to restrict entry and the Acts of 1962 and 1965 were retrograde steps.

Canada, Australia and New Zealand, as major immigrant countries, ought to change their present policies and allow in coloured Commonwealth immigrants on equal terms with white ones. And though, for a variety of historical reasons, the rich white countries are at present the targets for most criticism over matters of race—the European legacy in Africa is most obviously to blame here—this should not blind the countries of Asia, Africa and the West Indies to their own prejudices: minorities must be fully accepted and integrated; Chinese and Malay must accept each other as equal partners; West Indians who criticize Britain for limiting the number of their emigrants she will take should look again at their own parochial jealousies and restrictions.

The list of problems is endless; many of them are acute. Just because the Commonwealth contains representatives of most racial groups in the world as well as examples of nearly every kind of minority problem within its membership, it has the opportunity, possessed by no other group, to give a lead to the world in tackling this most explosive of issues. If it fails in this it will fail altogether.

CHAPTER 8

Future Prospects

MOST Commonwealth links, like the association itself, evolved out of the British Empire. They are important both for the advantages they provide each member and because they help maintain the Commonwealth connexion. But alone they are not a justification for the continued existence of the Commonwealth—that must be sought elsewhere. It is not enough merely to argue that something should continue because it happens to exist; better reasons in support of the Commonwealth's future than this must be found. The fact is that many Commonwealth links and perhaps, most notably, the economic ones discussed in this book would continue even were the Commonwealth to break up.

Common bonds—of habit, law, language, customs—are valuable assets which assist any process of co-operation; yet despite them the Commonwealth has no single international policies. Its members pursue their own defensive alliances; maintain non-alignment; and often find themselves on opposing sides of international issues. The most practical links giving exact advantages are those concerned with such matters as trade where ideological considerations have least influence.

As seen in this book Commonwealth economic co-operation may be conveniently divided into four fields of activity: trade; technical co-operation as in the maintenance of the sterling area; aid; and immigration.

Now, of these, it is arguable that trade is only marginally affected by Commonwealth membership. Naturally the close links of the association assist in making trade relations between member countries easier but of themselves they are neither responsible for the trade that is carried on, nor, as the example of South Africa amply demonstrates, would the pattern change significantly if the Commonwealth as such ceased to exist.

In the second area of technical economic co-operation—the maintenance of the sterling area—the picture is more confused. The sterling area on balance clearly does represent an asset to the Commonwealth as a whole and membership of it is of particular importance to those countries wishing to raise funds on the London capital market. British determination to preserve sterling, sometimes against enormous pressures, has often been interpreted as a sign of her belief in its practical advantage as a Commonwealth link and the feeling that the collapse of sterling would presage a collapse of the Commonwealth as well. This may have been true in the past and especially in the immediate post-war period when the United States showed little faith in sterling as an international currency. But this has hardly been the case during the 1960's. Apart from gold only the dollar and the pound are international currencies and increasingly, with growing pressures on the dollar and world demands for greater liquidity it has become more and more a matter of United States and European interest to support the pound; they do not want to see sterling collapse. Since this has become the case the interdependence of the Commonwealth and the sterling area has become less obvious: the disintegration of the Commonwealth would not necessarily mean either the collapse of sterling or the withdrawal of ex-Commonwealth countries from the sterling area.

The question of aid is highly complicated and it is often impossible to disentangle motives, or to determine which come first—Commonwealth links promoting greater aid or already existing interests ensuring that the greater part of British, Canadian, Australian and New Zealand aid goes to the Commonwealth anyway. Naturally, sentiment, past involvement and a continuing sense of British obligation to her one-time colonies make it easier for Britain and the other wealthier Commonwealth countries to direct aid into the Commonwealth rather than elsewhere; but it should not be forgotten that the existing links also represent long-standing interests and that arguments in support of British aid to East Africa would not alter significantly were countries such as Kenya to leave the Commonwealth.

Ironically, in the most explosive field of all—over immigration—appeals to sentiment and talk of Commonwealth links have been most frequently used, sometimes not without success. There is little doubt for example that but for the Commonwealth Britain would have restricted the flow of West Indians or Indians into the country long before she did; while Indian and West Indian appeals for Canada to relax her immigration laws would have had no success at all were it not for the Commonwealth connexion. Just because race issues involve such narrow-based prejudices of which their proponents are secretly ashamed, so any association that brings such people face to face on a so-called 'family' basis can exercise considerable powers of moral persuasion.

However, it has been the constant theme of this book that economic co-operation is a matter of self-interest. When the economic advantage of any one country is adversely affected by Commonwealth ties, then these would have to be very strong indeed or some practical alternative would have to be offered if an existing pattern were not to be changed. The amount of co-operation that does exist between Commonwealth countries is there because it suits them, not because of the Commonwealth as such. The political demise of the Commonwealth would not destroy the economic co-operation between members any more than its continuation will guarantee such co-operation in the face of other and stronger economic pulls from elsewhere.

A second theme has been that when a clash occurs between considerations of economic and political advantage, then the political factor will usually triumph. Thus no arguments of practical economics could save the Central African or West Indian federations when faced with nationalist pressures or racial questions of autonomy for the smaller groups; nor have the economic needs for greater numbers influenced policies based on prejudice where immigration is concerned.

Now it is against this background—harsh, cynical perhaps, but certainly true to life—and the normal behaviour of nations that Commonwealth prospects for the future must be judged. Constant reiteration of the predominance of self-interest in Commonwealth relations may appear to argue against any higher motives based upon idealism. Such is not the case. If anything, the Commonwealth has suffered because its supporters are too ready to defend it in terms of vague generalities while ignoring the toughly practical nature of the links that motivate any international grouping or alliance. Only when the mainly selfish nature of most national policies (of Commonwealth as much as other countries) is recognized does it then make sense to gauge the Commonwealth's future potential.

Observers of the Commonwealth scene have little difficulty pointing to the association's many weaknesses, while it is frequently argued that the whole Commonwealth experiment represents little more than an artificial left-over from Empire—a series of dwindling assets and steadily weakening bonds which should be allowed to fade away. The way Canada and Australia have come to rely increasingly upon the United States rather than Britain in matters of defence or trade; quarrels and tensions within the association—the Kashmir dispute between India and Pakistan, Central Africa and growing racial suspicions; or the progressive breakdown among African members of the Westminster style of two-party government as bequeathed by Britain—all tend to support such a view. Moreover, British cynics are not without justification when they assert that the only time Commonwealth countries attempt to co-operate at all is when by combination—appealing to sentiment and interest—they imagine they can force Britain's hand. All too rarely do Commonwealth countries appear to assert themselves in a more positive sense of trying as a united group to further less selfish international aims.

The very nature of the Commonwealth—its lack of central authority, the loosely binding and entirely free association of its members who all possess, at least in theory, equal rights (if not powers) can be misleading; furthermore, the fears of the weaker and smaller members that any attempt at close co-operation must inevitably lead to domination by Britain help to strengthen and project an image of a sometimes amiable, usually ineffective, potentially idealistic organization that is a good thing in theory though unlikely to work in practice. Unfortunately such negative thinking about the Commonwealth is to be found most frequently in Britain itself where the concept of a genuinely equal multiracial society seems least understood—or wanted. Thus, paradoxically, the country which most often claims credit for the Commonwealth idea is also the one providing its most persistent critics.

'Realistic' businessmen deride the sentimental links of the Commonwealth and want Britain to give up such nonsense for Europe where her future lies. Nostalgic imperialists who cannot accept a Commonwealth concept that allows black men from past colonies to sit as equals with whites pour angry scorn on the whole thing. A much larger mass of vague critics simply do not understand: though they realize and accept Britain's loss of world power they have yet to see what the alternatives are and to them the Commonwealth is no more than a watered-down and rather meaningless substitute for the much more tangible Empire. None of these groups can either see the Commonwealth's potential or grasp that a firm British lead on lines of a truly multiracial association could yet be her greatest contribution to world affairs.

If the Commonwealth is to survive in the future a new lead from Britain is essential. First because she is incomparably its most powerful and influential member; second, for past imperial reasons, because all the major Commonwealth links emanate from or pass through Britain. Remove her and the intricate network of ties and consultative machinery would fall apart. This is not to argue that Britain has a privileged position above her colleagues; the equal nature of the new association must be maintained and the onus should lie on all members to find a common purpose that justifies the organization. But as the most powerful it is right to expect the greatest efforts and concessions from Britain. If the Commonwealth is worth preserving in the future it is not because its individual members obtain particular advantages from it but because as an association it is capable of making a specific contribution of some kind to the world as a whole. All must strive to make such an effort; but, in power terms, the key role rests with Britain.

Now despite the nebulous nature of the Commonwealth association and the difficulty that even its most ardent supporters have to justify

COMMONWEALTH IN

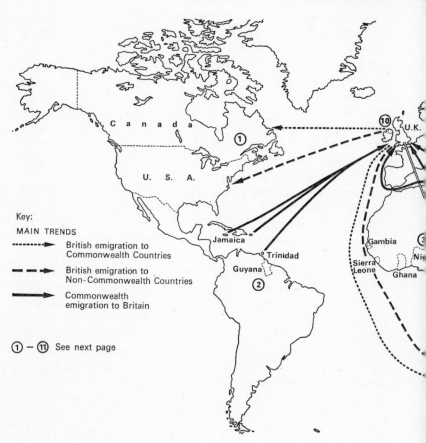

Key:

MAIN TRENDS

----▶ British emigration to
Commonwealth Countries

━ ━▶ British emigration to
Non-Commonwealth Countries

━━▶ Commonwealth
emigration to Britain

① – ⑪ See next page

RATION - MINORITIES

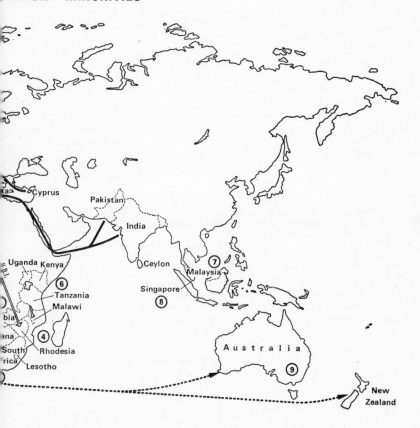

IMMIGRATION AND MINORITIES

1. CANADA. Occasional tensions between English- and French-speaking Canadians. A highly selective immigration policy that allows in few non-white immigrants.

2. GUYANA. 50% Indian population, the balance made up of 40% of African descent, Portuguese, Amerindians, Chinese and Europeans. Communal tensions; a special constitution giving proportional representation was devised before independence to safeguard the minority groups who feared Indian domination.

3. NIGERIA. Communal tensions as between the northern peoples (Hausa and Fulani) and the coastal peoples (Yoruba and Ibo) throughout 1966 cast doubt on the future of the present Federal system in Nigeria.

4. RHODESIA. With the declaration of UDI by the Smith Government the white settlers have made clear their intention of perpetuating their control over the African majority. The crisis threatens the whole future of the Commonwealth and of multiracialism in Africa.

5. ZAMBIA. Contains a European minority of about 70,000, mainly on the Copperbelt; they wield considerable economic power; the Government pursues a multiracial policy.

6. KENYA. Contains a European minority of about 60,000 and an Asian minority; tensions but the Government pursues a multiracial policy.

7. MALAYSIA. A Malay majority but substantial Chinese minority with great economic power; also a substantial Indian minority and in the Borneo countries of Sabah and Sarawak Dayak, Melanau and other minority groups as well. Malay fears of Chinese domination led to Singapore leaving the Federation.

8. SINGAPORE. Chinese majority (also Malays and Indians); left the Federation of Malaysia in 1965 due to Malay fears of Chinese economic and political domination.

9. AUSTRALIA. Highly selective immigration policy—'White Australia Policy'.

10. BRITAIN. The Commonwealth Immigration Acts of 1962 and 1965 restricted the flow of Commonwealth immigrants into Britain (in effect the Coloured ones).

11. SOUTH AFRICA. Although no longer in the Commonwealth still receives a considerable proportion of British emigrants. South African race attitudes (apartheid) are bound to have a continuing effect upon Commonwealth African approaches to racial questions.

it, all Britain's colonies on achieving independence seek membership and no country has left it voluntarily. The reason for this is twofold. First, membership of the Commonwealth does confer advantages of one kind or another upon the individual states which belong and these, despite criticisms, are sufficiently valuable that no country would willingly forgo them. Some, in the sphere of economic co-operation, we have already examined in detail; other benefits are to be found in the spheres of diplomacy, defence and a wide field of mutual consultation. Second, however uncertainly, Commonwealth countries do appear to recognize that the maintenance of the association does somehow offer long-term hopes for themselves and the world that none would willingly destroy—even if they are unable to define them. This vague awareness of values—of the need to preserve the association without obviously being able to say just why—is one of the more interesting political phenomena of the whole Commonwealth relationship. It comes out most clearly in a crisis. The near isolation of Britain during the 1966 Prime Ministers' Conference over Rhodesia might well have indicated a total breakdown of the Commonwealth and the walkout of the African members. Instead, without any clear statements as to why, even the countries most committed on the Rhodesian issue have made desperate efforts to avoid a breach. This can hardly be explained in terms of current diplomatic practice. It begins to make sense if one accepts as a thesis the possibility that all Commonwealth countries see wider world interests being served by the preservation of such an oddly assorted association. As Mrs Pandit once remarked, the strength of the Commonwealth lies in the association of so many 'unlike' peoples.

It is in this kind of thinking that a clue to the future may be found. What does the Commonwealth offer in a bigger sense than individual advantage for each member? What can the association achieve as a group that makes its preservation something all its members should strive to maintain? The answer to these questions must be sought in the widest field of international issues whose solution affects all nations.

There are four issues whose resolution can only be achieved by co-operation at the international level: world peace; poverty or the

overcoming of differences between rich and poor; overpopulation—
or tackling the question of population explosions; and coming to
terms with racial or colour differences.

These problems have to be faced against a revolutionary background that in many aspects is quite new. First, in a remarkably
short period of little more than half a generation the world has seen
the end of imperialism, at any rate in the nineteenth-century sense of
colonial empires. Second, for the first time in history, there has been
a general and momentous realization that poverty does not have to be
the lot of the majority of mankind: that modern techniques of
development can be applied to all societies so that even a poor
country with few resources may achieve a minimum standard of
living for the whole population. This realization that poverty can be
overcome by modern techniques is a unique event of the twentieth
century. In developing countries it is represented by the revolutions
of expectations: the determination of governments to modernize, the
insistence of the people upon quick change; in the rich countries its
recognition has been acknowledged, however tentatively, by their
participation in aid programmes. Third, the emergence of the non-
aligned world and the insistence of a great number of weak countries
that they will not simply be pawns have created a quite new international situation. By associating together, however loosely, in order
to resist the power blandishments of the two sides in the Cold War
the poor and underdeveloped have for the first time laid claims to
acknowledgement as a group in their own right.

Coupled with the possibilities of nuclear destruction that no one
can ignore, these new revolutions, all emanating from the weaker
members of the world community, together serve to remind us that
we belong to a single world whose problems can no longer be solved
in isolation—all are concerned. The first halting steps towards a
system of world government taken by the United Nations, international aid programmes, and the recognition by the great powers
that their differences can no longer be solved by warfare together
constitute a hesitant acceptance of a new one-world society that must
increasingly dominate international politics.

A vague realization of world interdependence is one thing; and practical steps to make it more effective are something quite different. To date world successes in this field have been severely limited: the United Nations only just manages to survive as a world body; and most issues are still settled, if at all, on the old basis of power politics. Even so, any joint attempts by groups of nations to solve their differences and problems represents a genuine advance.

It is at this point that the potential of the Commonwealth becomes so important. As a group of nations with the advantages that the habit of association and the links it possesses give to it, the Commonwealth is still small enough to achieve results in many fields where the world body of the United Nations is too large and unwieldy. Moreover, the Commonwealth contains among its members a microcosm of most world differences and problems. It includes countries at both extremes of wealth—the very rich, such as Britain, Canada and Australia, and the very poor, such as India, Pakistan and Tanzania; apart from the super powers, Britain at one end represents great power strength and influence, Malta or Trinidad at the other are examples of small, at least semi-dependent, territories, while in between Canada and Australia stand for the wealthy middle powers and India for major influence in the non-aligned world. Problems of poverty, development and population explosion are all to be found among its members; so is virtually every kind of political system and attitude to world problems (apart from Communism) from the right wing Cold War alignment of a country such as Australia, through the more temperate gradations of approach to be found in Britain or Canada, to the positions at the other end of the scale taken by India or Tanzania. In India extreme poverty as well as the population explosion have to be faced on a massive scale. While amongst all members there are differences sometimes amounting to quarrels that demand the greatest diplomatic tact to prevent them from developing into breaches of a more dangerous nature. Finally, all the variations of race, colour and creed whose emphasis threatens world security are to be found within the Commonwealth.

Despite the huge size of the Commonwealth, with a population of nearly 800 million, its present total of 23* independent members does represent a working group more likely to discover common solutions to problems than the wider organization of the United Nations. Since the Commonwealth contains examples of all the main international problems it should try to tackle them on a joint basis; and if it can begin to find solutions where the world is still groping this will be its justification.

It is convenient to divide the most obvious international issues into four (see above): the maintenance of peace; the achievement of economic progress by the developing countries—or their breakthrough to self-sustained growth; the containment of the population explosion; and the avoidance of a world split along colour lines. Apart from nuclear war the greatest danger arises out of the possibility that racial and colour differences will divide it into two groups: the rich white and the rest. The prospect of a world split along these lines is now very close; unfortunately its imminence is all too little realized.

A brief examination of these four areas indicates most clearly where the Commonwealth's most effective contribution can be made. Over the question of war the world appears—just—to have recognized the enormity of taking such a step in order to solve outstanding differences. The Cuban crisis of 1962 made both sides see as they had not done till then how totally disastrous a nuclear confrontation would prove, not only to the direct antagonists but to the world at large. The responsibility for averting world and nuclear war must rest with the major powers.

On the second issue—however imperfectly—there has been an admission by the rich countries that they have an obligation towards the greater part of the world to help the process of development. Aid, whatever the motives for giving it, has come to stay as a feature of international relations. Here the Commonwealth (see above, pages 120–130) can give a real lead; certainly its rich members can achieve far more than they have so far managed to do. At any rate the world has recognized the problem and is beginning to come to grips with it.

---

* Bechuanaland and Basutoland have now attained independence as Botswana and Lesotho, also Barbados, bringing the total to 26.

Similarly, despite difficulties arising out of religious scruples, ignorance and the sheer speed of growth, the greatest problems connected with the population explosion are in fact of a technical nature. They have been recognized, and no doubt in time—probably only just in time—they will be overcome.

Of all world problems those of racial and colour differences present the most intractable and explosive possibilities. Where colour is concerned reason is most easily replaced by prejudice and common sense and humane solutions ignored in favour of those which support racial arrogance. Such attitudes are not confined to the Commonwealth; they are universal. But there are more than enough racial and colour differences, problems of minorities and deep-seated prejudices within the Commonwealth to make this issue the one on which the whole association could founder. Certainly the ideal of a multiracial Commonwealth is a noble one; and the Commonwealth cannot survive if it abandons the concept. At the time of writing the Commonwealth Prime Ministers' Conference of 1966 has devoted almost all its attention to the question of Rhodesia and many observers have been surprised that the organization has somehow avoided breaking up over this issue. The dangers of a world split along colour lines are very great and whether such a division can be avoided may well depend upon the eventual solution that Britain works out to the UDI crisis. Should narrow prejudice, arguments of white solidarity, 'kith and kin' be allowed to triumph, then a disastrous lining up of peoples according to their colour will inevitably follow. Nothing could be more dangerous or give rise to greater bitterness than such a world division. Moreover, since the white races represent a minority—and a small one at that—the long-term results of a colour split, however much the white peoples might hold their own for a time due to their wealth and more advanced development, could only prove a disaster to them. Therefore, if only for the most selfish reasons of their own future preservation, the onus now lies upon the white nations—the leading powers of today—to come to terms with a world in which before very long they will not only find themselves even more outnumbered than at present but relatively less powerful as well.

It is in this field of race relations that the greatest challenge to the Commonwealth lies. As a group the Commonwealth contains examples of most races and colours while all racial problems are abundantly represented within its membership and as between one country and another. It is idle to assume that less prejudice exists among Commonwealth countries than in the world at large. But at least the habit of co-operation and the avowed ideal of a multiracial association gives to the Commonwealth the opportunity to tackle this most vexed and explosive of issues in a way no other group can. Somehow Commonwealth advantages must be harnessed to solving questions of racial antagonisms. Certainly, if the Commonwealth fails to find a way for its various members—and particularly those countries containing minority groups—to learn first tolerance and then acceptance of each other on a genuine basis of equality, there is little hope that any other world organization will succeed.

This possibility is recognized in the Commonwealth though as yet not much progress has been achieved. Perhaps the realization that as a group it has more chances of solving racial issues than any other world body accounts for the extraordinary flexibility of the Commonwealth and its survival through the various crises it periodically faces. Both the expulsion of South Africa and the determined pressure of most members upon Britain over Rhodesia indicate how Commonwealth countries are reluctant to lose one of the few remaining chances of effective international action over race questions.

This book has been concerned with problems of economic co-operation and an attempt has been made to demonstrate two things: first that Commonwealth links are mainly the result of past imperial ties, and Commonwealth countries continue to maintain them because it is in their interest to do so. Second, that these links in themselves are not sufficient reason for the Commonwealth's existence; they help to bind the organization together and as such are useful instruments of policy. But a long-term justification of the Commonwealth must be found in the pursuit of some common purpose. Of all major problems, that of race relations presents most difficulties and, potentially, faces the world community with the most explosive and ugly possibilities. The multiracial composition and nature of the Commonwealth gives to the association greater advantages for tackling this question than any other group of nations possesses. If in the years ahead the Commonwealth can face its own racial issues with honesty and find genuine solutions to them it need look for no other reason to justify its existence. The greatest service the Commonwealth can render to the world is to put into practice the concept of a truly multiracial society.

Bibliography

THERE is a vast amount of writing on Commonwealth subjects. The books listed below are no more than a short selective list: a few are general, giving historical or modern background; most deal more specifically with particular subjects such as aid.

ARNOLD, GUY, *Towards Peace and a Multiracial Commonwealth*, Chapman & Hall, 1964.

BENHAM, F., *Economic Aid to Underdeveloped Countries*, Oxford University Press, 1961.

BLOOMFIELD, PAUL, *Edward Gibbon Wakefield*, Longmans, 1961.

HANCOCK, SIR KEITH, *Survey of British Commonwealth Affairs 1918–1939 (Volume II. Problems of Economic Policy)*, Oxford University Press, 1942.

HOBSON, J. A., *Imperialism, a Study*, George Allen & Unwin Ltd., 1902 (reprinted 1954).

INGRAM, DEREK, *Commonwealth for a Colour-Blind World*, George Allen & Unwin Ltd., 1965.

KNAPLUND, PAUL, *Britain, Commonwealth and Empire, 1901–1955*, Hamish Hamilton, 1956.

LITTLE, I. M. D. and CLIFFORD, J. M., *International Aid*, George Allen & Unwin Ltd., 1965.

MANSERGH, NICHOLAS, *et al.*, *Commonwealth Perspectives*, Duke University Press, 1958.

OVERSEAS DEVELOPMENT INSTITUTE (the Institute is primarily concerned with all aspects of British aid to developing countries; below are listed a few of its publications most relevant to the subject of this book).
British Aid—Survey and Comment.
British Aid—Technical Assistance.
British Aid—Colonial Development.

Aid to the West Indies.

British Private Investment in East Africa.

Aid in the Commonwealth.

SHONFIELD, ANDREW, *The Attack on World Poverty*, Chatto & Windus, 1960.

SOPER, TOM, *Evolving Commonwealth*, Pergamon, 1965.

WARD, BARBARA, *The Rich Nations and the Poor Nations*, CBC, Toronto, 1961.

WILLIAMSON, JAMES A., *A Short History of British Expansion* (2 volumes), *The Old Colonial Empire, The Modern Empire and Commonwealth*, Macmillan & Co. Ltd., 1922 (reprinted 1961).

Index

Aden 44
  build-up of military base 50
Africa
  British colonization 5
  distribution of industries 113
  independence of colonies 41–3
  neo-colonialism in 133
  shortages of trained personnel 113
Aid 29–40, 98–130
  American 109
  attitudes of recipients 104–5
  Cold War as stimulus for 30,
    101
  in the Commonwealth 102
  Communist 109
  motives of donors 99–101, 104
  political 101, 102
  from self-interest 101–2
  for world stability 102
Australia
  aid to Commonwealth countries
    119
  aid to Pacific territories 50
  ANZUS defence pact 25, 53, 93
  demand for reciprocal prefer-
    ences 14
  foreign investment in 74–5
  meat, British preference for 65
  protection of home industries 8
  trade with Britain 60
  trade with N. Zealand 66
  'White Australia' Policy 154,
    160, 168

Baghdad Pact, establishment of 24
Basutoland 49, 134
  independence of 43

Bechuanaland 49
  economic problems 114, 115
  independence of 43, 134
Botswana 43, 134
Britain
  aid to Commonwealth countries
    30–5, 43–6, 48–9, 118
  Commonwealth immigrants
    150–1, 152, 168
  costs of overseas bases 24
  decolonization by 28–9, 40–50
  defence costs 23–4
  emigration to Commonwealth
    countries 146
  financial crises 16, 19, 67–9, 73
  financing of colonial development
    31–5
  'interests' in former colonies 133
  leading role in Commonwealth
    21, 24, 25, 165
  neo-colonialism in Africa, accusa-
    tions of 133, 136
  overseas investment 72, 74–9
  post-war economic weakness
    20–1, 22, 68
  protection of gold reserves 18
  war loans to 21, 33
British Guiana
  independence of 90
  trade with Britain 61
British Somaliland, independence of
  42
Burma, independence outside
  Commonwealth 27

Canada
  aid to Commonwealth countries
    119

Canada—*cont.*
  aid to W. Indies 49–50, 123
  defence pact with USA
    (NORAD) 25, 92
  demand for reciprocal
    preferences 14
  economic ties with USA 22,
    25, 75, 91
  foreign investment in 75
  immigration policy 153, 160, 168
  protection of home industries 7,
    8
  trade with USA 15, 60, 65
Central African Federation
  British investment in 45–6
  dissolution 43, 45
  political failure 45
Central banks in Commonwealth
  countries 72
Ceylon
  as Commonwealth member 27,
    41
  resources 113
  trade with Britain 61
  trade with India and Pakistan 66
CHAMBERLAIN, J. 7, 8, 9
  tariff reform proposals 9
CHURCHILL, opposition to Indian
  independence 26
Cold War
  Commonwealth alliances during
    24
  pressures on British economy 16
Colombo Plan 31, 35–40, 102
  as channel for technical aid 36–7
  extension to non-Commonwealth
    countries 36
  interests of non-Asian members
    36
  mode of operation 37–8
Colonial Development Act, 1929
  31
Colonial Development and
  Welfare Acts
  1940 32
  1945 33
Colonial Development and Welfare
  Corporation 31

Colonies
  aid to British war effort 33
  budgetary expenses of 31
  dependent 49
  economic strengths of 43–4
  as markets and sources of supply
    11
  self-government in 5, 8
Committee on Commercial and
  Industrial Policy, Final Report
  of 11, 12–13
Commodity agreements 124
Common Market 83–9
  British attempts at membership
    85–9
  growing economic strength 53
  trade with Commonwealth
    countries 59, 62, 65, 66
Commonwealth
  advantages of membership 52
  aid-donor members 30, 104
  capital needs of 74–6
  growing membership 41, 43,
    173
  inclusion of Asian members
    26–7, 41
  migrating population 148–9
  multiracial, ideal of 173
  political evolution since 1945
    51–2
  racialism 147–8
Commonwealth aid 102–30
  consultative bodies 117
  general problems 114–16
  grants 106
  loans 106
  main donors 104, 109, 118–20
  main recipients 118
  to member states 110
  need for planned effort 120–30
  requirements of members
    111–16
  technical assistance and training
    106–7, 118
  trade concessions 108
  to UN agencies 110
Commonwealth Aid Council,
  suggested 127–30

Commonwealth Immigration Act,
  1962 151–2
Commonwealth Sugar Agreement
  65, 108, 124
Commonwealth trade 57–67
  Britain's role as market 58, 59
  commodity agreements 65
  effects of diversification 63, 66
  investment patterns 76
  patterns of 61–7
  statistics for 1956 59
  statistics for 1964 62–3
  trade with non-members 57–8,
    59, 62, 63
  wheat preference abolished 64
Congo, independence struggles 42
Cyprus
  aid requirements 114
  run-down of military base 50

Dominions Royal Commission,
  report of 11–12

East Africa
  proposed 'common market' 95
  trade between states 66
  trade with Britain 60
Economic blocs 80–97
  Common Market 83–9
  EFTA 85
  regional trading groups 94–7
  USA 89–94
Economics and world politics 25
EFTA 85
  trade with Commonwealth
    countries 62, 63
Emigration to Dominions 22,
  146–7, 149

Fiji, future of 44
First World War 5–6, 10–13
France, independence of African
  colonies 42
Free trade 6, 7

Gambia, British support of 43,
  62, 114
Ghana
  aid for Volta development
    scheme 113
  as Commonwealth member 41,
    42
  economic viability 43
  independence of 40, 41
  Nkrumah overthrown 134
  trade with Britain 60, 66
Guyana
  minority groups in population
    168
  trade with Britain and Canada
    66

Imperial Economic Conference
  (1923) 13, 14
Imperial preference 6, 8, 13–17
Independence of colonial territories
  40–50
  economic considerations 43–50
India
  aid requirements 28, 109–10, 112
  aid, total receipts 117–18
  attitude to Britain after indepen-
    dence 27
  British trade with 27–8
  as Commonwealth member 27,
    41
  Five-Year Development Plans 28
  importance to Britain 26
  independence of 16–17, 26
  industrial establishment 112
  non-alignment policy 28
  trade with Ceylon and Pakistan
    66
  withdrawal of sterling balances
    from Britain 28

Jamaica
  incentives to N. American inves-
    tors 76
  industrial development 114
  natural reserves 47

Jamaica—*cont.*
trade with Britain   61
withdrawal from W. Indies Federation   47
Japan, trade with Commonwealth countries   60, 62, 63, 66

Kenya
abandonment of military base   50
agricultural development   113
British aid to   103
independence of   42–3
Mau Mau troubles   42, 155
white minority   155, 168

Lease-Lend, conclusion of   23
Lesotho   43, 134
Loans   *see under* Aid
Loans to colonial governments   31–2

Malawi   43
dependence on Britain   46, 114
imports from Rhodesia   61
trade with Britain   61
trade with neighbours   66
Malaya
attitude to Singapore   48
as Commonwealth member   41
in Federation of Malaysia   48
independence of   40, 41, 43
tin and rubber industries   113
Malaysia, Federation of   48
gold and dollar reserves   72
member states   48
minority groups in population   168
problem of Indonesian confrontation   115
trade with Britain   61
Malta
British support of   43, 48
opposition to dockyard run-down   50
Marshall Aid to Europe   23, 29, 98
Mauritius, future of   44

Middle East, British involvement in   4
Military bases, British   50–1
Minorities, racial   155–8
Monarch as head of Commonwealth   27

NEHRU, P.   27
Neo-colonialism   131–43
British activities in Africa   133, 136
developing countries, fears of   137, 143
expatriate assistance, financial and technical   140–1
New Zealand
aid to Commonwealth countries   119
aid to Pacific territories   50, 119
ANZUS defence pact   25, 53
immigrant policy   154, 160
meat and dairy products   5, 60–1, 65
trade with Australia   66
trade with Britain   60
Nigeria
aid for oil prospecting   113
Federal Government overthrown (1966)   134
independence of   42
trade with Britain   60, 66
tribal friction   168
NKRUMAH
overthrow of   134
role in African politics   41–2
Northern Rhodesian in Central African Federation   45
Nyasaland
in Central African Federation   45
dependence on Britain   46

Overseas Food Corporation   33

Pakistan
aid requirements   112

Pakistan—*cont.*
  as Commonwealth member 27, 41
  resources 113
  trade with Britain 61
  trade with Ceylon and India 66
Pan-Africanism 95, 96, 97
Protectionism 7–10, 14

Rhodesia
  sanctions against 46, 134
  support from S. Africa 134
  trade with Britain 60, 62
  trade with neighbours 66, 72
  UDI crisis 43, 46, 134, 156, 168, 173
Russia as major world power 20

St. Helena, future of 44
Second World War 16
  post-war economic situation 20–1
Self-sufficiency, imperial 12, 13
Sierra Leone
  independence of 42
  trade with Britain 60, 66
Singapore
  Chinese minority 168
  as military base 50–1
  withdrawal from Malaysian Federation 48
South Africa
  departure from Commonwealth 42
  goods boycotted 56
  opposition to black African countries 41, 42
  position in Commonwealth Africa 134
  racial policy 134, 168
Southern Rhodesia in Central African Federation 45
  see also Rhodesia
Statute of Westminster, 1931 10, 13
Sterling 17–19

Sterling area 18, 67, 69–73, 162
  benefits of membership 69, 73
  controls 72
  maintenance of 73
Sterling Bloc (1931) 18
Sterling crises 67–9, 73
Students from Commonwealth countries 158–9
Swaziland 49

Tanganyika
  British aid to 103
  groundnuts project 31, 33, 34, 35
  independence of 42
'Tanzam' railway scheme 103
Tanzania 134
Tariffs, imperial, against foreign goods 14
Trinidad
  incentives to N. American investors 76
  industrial development 114
  trade with Britain 61
  withdrawal from W. Indies Federation 47
Tristan da Cunha, future of 44

Uganda
  independence of 42
  Kabaka deposed (1966) 134
United Africa Company 33
United Nations' administration of aid 110–11
USA
  aid to India 93
  aid programmes 109
  control of Canadian industries 91
  defence pacts 25, 53, 89–90
  interest in Australia 92–3
  investment in Canada 75, 90
  involvement 90
  as major world power 20, 89
  post-war economic strength 22–3, 53
  trade with Commonwealth countries 59, 62, 63, 65

West Indies
  Federation experiment   46–7
  smaller islands   43, 47, 114
  trade with Britain   60, 61, 66
  trade with Canada   66
West Indies Federation, breakdown
  of   47
West Indies Royal Commission
  (1938)   32
World economic depression   14
  effects on dependent colonies   15

Zambia
  British preferences discontinued
    64
  copper industry   113
  effects of Rhodesian crisis   46,
    115, 134
  gold and dollar reserves   72
  imports from Rhodesia   62, 66,
    72
  trade with Britain   61
  white minority   155, 168